Classic Car
ADVENTURES

**Featuring old car tales from enthusiasts:
Anglias, Bentleys, Bugattis & *Cortinas*
to *Datsuns, Ferraris, MGs* & many more!**

RICHARD McCANN

CONTENTS

FOREWORD

I must confess to knowing very little about cars. When Richard McCann began writing his motoring column for OVL Magazine ten years ago, I thought his articles would go over my head. How wrong I was. Witty and knowledgeable, Richard is passionate about all things auto-related and his ability to connect with his readers ensures that his popular column is loved by both petrolheads and car novices like me.

The same can be said for Richard's collection of classic car adventures. While they are undeniably appealing to motoring enthusiasts, they inevitably attract a much wider audience. For surely we all have fond (or sometimes otherwise) memories of car journeys while growing up, holidaying, exploring or just taking a leisurely drive for the fun of it.

The fascinating stories that Richard has uncovered are certain to entertain. An intrepid trip to Italy over the Alps in a 1960s Ford Anglia will fill you with awe while other tales will make you chuckle, such as the childhood memory of travelling in a Triumph Herald and spotting one of its wheels overtaking on the road. This engaging collection captures the excitement and uncertainty of motoring at a time when vehicles, roads and laws were quite different from today.

My own classic car adventures are much less impressive. Nevertheless they are very happy memories when car journeys often felt like an adventure. A tedious traffic jam on the M25 *en route* to the airport didn't feature in my childhood holidays. Instead our camping trips to Devon began in the middle of the night as my parents thought it easier to travel with three sleeping children. I still remember the excitement of being lifted into the back of our Morris Traveller in my sleeping bag, the seats folded down (something we couldn't do nowadays with seat belt legislation) and the camping gear and dog squeezed in between us. I would keep my eyes tightly shut, not wanting to spoil the magic, while listening to my parents talking in hushed tones or what we referred to as their 'holiday voices'. Later a large bar of Dairy Milk would be shared while singing to pass the time. The Bubble Car Song was a particular favourite: *'Beep beep, beep beep, his horn went beep beep beep!'* we trilled with cheeks crammed full of chocolate chunks.

When Richard told me about his idea for this book, I knew he was on to a winner. What a brilliant inspiration! I mentioned it to a few people and every one of them proceeded to tell me their favourite old car tale, each one bringing a twinkle to their eye and a smile to their face. Never mind a dog, over the years our cars really did become part of the family: a companion we relied upon to help us follow our dreams and take us on new adventures.

I'm certain that this book will be enjoyed by many but I have a feeling it won't stop here. I am in no doubt that there are countless classic car adventures just waiting to be told.

Jacqui Hagen

EDITOR, OVL MAGAZINE

INTRODUCTION

During the past few decades the values of classic cars have skyrocketed.

Many popular models are now priced well beyond the reach of most regular enthusiasts, unless they were fortunate enough to own – or have access to – classic cars when they were little more than cheap transport for youngsters and eccentrics!

This book brings together tales, not of investors and playboys, but of ordinary 'car people'. Call them what you will: Petrolheads, car guys (and gals), Gearheads ... we all know what we are and we can recognise a fellow 'sufferer' in seconds.

There are stories here of help from mums and dads, of wings fixed with filler, and engines botched together just well enough to survive another week's motoring.

There are stories of intrepid foreign adventures, of racing, sprinting, rallying, and just plain getting down and oily with the machines we love.

So fold down that main screen, adjust the little 'Aeros', stick on your goggles and join us for a high-octane ride from the past to the present!

MG ADVENTURES

BY CHARLES BOULTON

"A trip to remember, always ..."

Charles was fortunate to grow up in the heart of the Cotswolds with a car-mad father and uncle. The two men had many cars over the years, from Jaguars to Bugattis, and MGs were an enduring passion.

Right up to the '70s, Charles's father was buying new MGs – the last of which (a RWA round-wheel-arch Midget) Charles later spotted parked up and persuaded the lady owner to sell it to him for old time's sake.

But the first of the Boulton family MGs was a pre-War model that – by a process of deduction by Charles – was probably one of the early 4-seat touring 1 ½ litre models that the company started producing in the '30s. Fitted with a sporting 4-cylinder twin-carburettor engine yet only a diminutive 1548cc churning out a very respectable for the time 54 bhp.

With a lightweight ash wood-framed body and metal skin, the two seat MGs might have got up to speeds approaching 100 mph flat out given enough space, but the four-seater version was aimed at the sporty driver who now had a family to transport. Yet with the folding screen in the 'flat' position it would still see more than 80mph! And in a motor car with a live rear axle, beam up front and half-elliptic springs all round – especially with a full complement of

1960s Mk II Jaguar driven by Charles's father with Charles as co-pilot

passengers and a flapping hood – that was plenty to push the skinny tyres and the drum brakes to their limits!

Charles takes up the story:

I was eight or nine years old and it was the first holiday I can really ever remember going on. Must have been the '60s. We lived up Cleeve Hill near Cheltenham and my father had a four seater MG convertible at the time. This was a pre-War car – spare tyre on the back, two cut-away doors, hinged at the back and prone to fly open when the body flexed over bumps, so often known as 'suicide doors' since you stood a good chance of falling out! Tall 19 inch wire wheels.

Dad had bought this racy old MG because, despite its small size, it was a four seater instead of a two-seater like most sports MGs. Or at least, it claimed to be a four seater!

Dad had been using this little car for local trips, but one day he announced that he was taking us all on holiday and that I was to help

Some of the Boulton family's many immaculate MGs

The '30s MG was regarded as an old car even back then – but still
sought-after by sporting motorists as the last of the 'true' MGs!

pack because we were leaving at TWO O'CLOCK IN THE MORNING! Two o'clock? I'd never been up at that time – the middle of the night. It was just so exciting. And where were we going? To some place I'd never heard of in a county called Cornwall.

To be precise, we were going to a place called Par Sands, six miles from St Austell and more than 250 miles from home! Even today, that's a heck of a drive, well over three hours at constant high speed in a fast car on the M5 motorway. But back then, in a car that would have probably been past its best some 25 years earlier, it was an intrepid adventure – especially with a full load on board.

And boy was it loaded! Mum and Dad took everything we were going to need for a two-week seaside holiday. And I mean everything. Cases of clothes, beach things, and of course since it was self-catering and my parents had no idea what facilities were nearby, we also took all our food for a fortnight. Plus I certainly wasn't going without my bicycle, so that was lashed on to the spare wheel that in turn was strapped to the tall slab petrol tank at the back.

An early start!

Two o'clock in the morning duly arrived and off we set in total darkness, the tiny lights of the MG guiding our path on the old country roads towards Bristol and beyond. There was of course no motorway, so we probably struck off to the south towards Cirencester before heading west through Tetbury.

Dad had been driving this overloaded motor expedition for a couple of hours or so and we were around Bristol, so he was making terrific progress. The hood was still up and we were pretty chilly in there, with no proper windows and certainly no heater! As I said, it was pretty cramped in there, mum and dad up front, and me in the back surrounded by cases of clothes and bags of provisions sufficient to last a family for 14 days, plus tools and spares for the car and my bike hanging off the back with the spare wheel. It was totally full of – well, you name it, really ... and all on those four inch wide tyres on the tall skinny wheels, the little old engine doing its best for mile after mile.

As dawn started to break, dad stopped and lowered the hood – daytime had been declared and we were off to the seaside! It wasn't really light enough or warm enough for top-down motoring but that's how a sporting motorist travelled back then and of course while mum and dad were protected by the windscreen, I caught all the draft in the back. But what the heck, I simply snuggled down amongst the luggage and enjoyed the ride.

Embarrassment

And what a ride – dad was really going for it ... we were passing car after car! Now, with all that weight and the car's little engine and considerably over-stretched brakes, not too much was going to be slow enough to get in our way, so we didn't often need to risk an overtake on those country lanes, but now suddenly we were overtaking a whole line of cars in one go!

This was fast motoring, I thought. Dad was in the middle of the road and we were steaming by maybe 20, 30 or more vehicles. 'What's happening dad?' I shouted from the back. 'Why are we overtaking everyone?'

'We're not overtaking,' said dad, 'they're all parked!' Parked? But they all had people sitting in them? It was at that precise moment that we all saw the temporary traffic lights glowing red. Yes, maybe half a mile of stationery traffic had all been waiting patiently at roadworks for a green light. They must have been waiting for ages, when suddenly, right up to the head of the queue without any waiting at all, or even slowing down, comes us, bound for the seaside and keen to make progress!

How embarrassing! We'd flashed past the lot, straight up to the front. I went very quiet and poor Dad had no choice but to sit at the head of the queue, doubtless avoiding eye contact with anyone until the light finally changed to green and then, with a wave of thanks, he gunned the poor little car and off we set in front of everyone, which I'm sure delighted all the patient drivers as they then finally moved off themselves, only to enjoy the prospect of spending the rest of their journey behind us.

The first 10 hours are the toughest. Maybe

So it gets towards lunchtime, and we're *still* going. It's been around 10 hours now. TEN HOURS! And the poor little MG is still humming away. Terrific cars, MGs. Then we suddenly start weaving around the road. A puncture!

By this time we're on a main holiday route to Cornwall and it's busy. Traffic is streaming past us and dad had done his best to pull us as close to the verge as possible so that we're not too much in the way while still giving himself a bit of room to change the wheel. But first, he needs his tools, so out comes all the family. And the luggage. And the food.

All that careful packing, using every inch of space, is for nothing as the whole lot is scattered across the grass verge. And there's the bottle jack and the centre lock hammer. Dad positions the jack, and up goes the car, a few belts from the wheel hammer and the racing-style centre lock spins off followed by the punctured tyre as the wheel is slid off its splined hub.

Poor dad then goes around to the back of the car, where of course he starts untying my bike before he can get down to unstrapping the spare wheel and tyre from the fuel tank. The spare is wheeled around to the front, slid on the hub, followed by the centre lock spinner which is hammered up tight so there's no chance of it coming loose.

As mum and I then start unceremoniously bundling all our things from the grass back in the car – not quite so neatly packed this time – dad puts the flat tyre and wheel back in its straps on the tank, and my bike is lashed to the wheel again, all the time dodging the coast-bound traffic whizzing past really close, as I start to wonder if we'll ever get our lunch. After 10 hours on the road, it's already been a long day.

Finally, before we all pile back in, dad unwinds the bottle jack and moves to store it with the rest of the tools. It's at this point, as the weight of the car is transferred to the wheel, that Dad sees the perished old inner tube fail. The spare tyre is now also flat ...

I think the people in Cornwall – and maybe back in Gloucestershire too – probably heard the collective groan from all of us. There was nothing else for it ... mother was elected to stay with the car, and dad and I set out walking, with dad carrying the punctured tyre and wheel. At least it was sunny.

My father guessed the direction of where the nearest garage might be and after what seemed like an age, we found a place. Way back then, there were very few specialist tyre places, and any roadside garage would fix a puncture for you. But not usually while you waited! So we hung around. After all, we had little choice and nothing else to do. Meanwhile, poor mum was at the roadside, traffic rushing by, still waiting, and not knowing when we might return.

Eventually one of the mechanics became free and they soon had the tyre off the wheel, the inner tube in water, located the puncture, dried it, roughed up the rubber and glued on a patch. Then all back on the wheel and inflated. Mended! Ah yes, then it was the long walk all the way back, but at least I could play hooping the wheel along this time so dad didn't have to carry it. Finally we turned the corner and saw the MG, with mum bored witless and dusty from an hour or so sitting at the side of a very busy, noisy road watching the traffic. On when the wheel, all good this time, jack and tools packed away and – lunchtime now a distant memory – we were back on the road again!

Late night. And still motoring

It was almost nightfall when we rolled into Par Sands.

Par Sands in Cornwall

After almost 300 miles in a very long day in the little MG and – so far as I could tell as a youngster – it didn't miss a beat. That engine still sounded as good as ever to my eight-year old ears and one can hardly blame the puncture on the MG. Small wonder people love MGs so much to this day.

But although we were now close to our holiday home, we had yet to find it. Remember that back then we didn't choose holidays from glossy brochures or websites. There were no colour photos to look through and satnavs to guide you right to the door of a house in an unfamiliar town. My father might have seen a local newspaper advert and written in, or maybe he heard about the accommodation from a friend of a friend. That's how it was. So we didn't know what we were going to see until we found it.

Aha ...

A beach hut was not what Charles and his family expected for their holiday home

The MG's headlights illuminated what was literally a large beach hut. A wooden hut. On the beach. A hut that you were allowed to sleep in. But it's still a beach hut. Half way across the inside of the hut someone had put two curtains and behind those were two bunk beds. This was our home for two weeks.

In defence of the place, it was cosy, and although it was even smaller than the caravans of the time, there was a little camping gas stove in there, and we were our own bosses – remember that in the '60s any family staying in Bed-and-Breakfast accommodation had to be all up, dressed and outside on the street by 9-30 at the latest – no matter what the weather! And you were not allowed back in the place until time for dinner and bed!

Cornwall's answer to the Dead Sea

Par Sands is very close to St Austell and that's where the English China Clay Company had its factory. Of course it couldn't possibly happen now, but back then in those more *laissez-faire* times the factory thought it was a good idea to discharge all its waste clay into the Bay of this popular coastal beauty spot.

And no-one felt that was anything that they should object to!

Charles exploring the district on what appears to be a very shiny bicycle!

So there I was on our first morning in the hut, and anxious both to escape the wooden shed and to get across the sands and into the sea. It was a long run to the 'tide out' point, and when I made it I ran straight in.

Aarrrgggh – instead of the waves that I expected it was just like walking through two feet of mud.

I plodded back all the way across the sands to my parents on the long walk of shame, considerably less enthusiastic than my outward run to the sea, and covered from head to foot in clay slime. It was like the photos of people covering themselves in Dead Sea mudpacks. Except this certainly wasn't voluntary, and neither I nor my poor parents were able to think of any redeeming features. So there I was, living in a hut on a beach, next to the sea and yet not allowed to go near the water.

A Bugatti arrives!

Now that the chief attraction of this beach holiday had been shut down to me so soon, it was a great excitement when my Uncle John arrived, having decided to take a run out in his Bugatti racing car – terribly glamorous!

Uncle John was father to my cousin Mike, who was later to become a regular racer himself for many years in sports cars such as Bentleys and TVRs and who now marshals at the Bugatti Club's Prescott Hill Climb, so the family tradition continues to this day!

A sporting pre-War Bugatti of the type popular in Charles's family

The family MGA

The excitement of having Uncle John joining us for the second week was diluted a little by the fact that there was now one extra person to squeeze into the beach hut! And just as the four of us settled down to talk about our journeys – and the clay mud – there was a bolt of lightning outside that lit up the bay, followed by a clap of thunder. Down came the rain.

Except this was not just any rain. It wasn't even just a massive cloud-burst. It was an epic storm that flash-flooded everything.

The sturdy Cornish houses weren't built to withstand a freak storm of this magnitude, so it was little wonder that a primitive wooden beach hut stood no chance.

We sat looking with amazement as the water poured through our roof and soaked all our possessions, while outside the MG and the Bugatti filled with water like two exotic sporting bathtubs.

Dad turned on our battery-powered radio, and we all sat listening to the announcer tell the world that *'The freak storm and floods had hit the holiday resort of Par Sands'*. Yes, we were in a beach hut in the place that had actually made it on to BBC national news!

Still racing ...

That was my first long distance road trip and my first holiday experience. Everything was loaded, wringing wet, back into the little MG and we set off for home. And after a long but thankfully uneventful journey we all made it safely back to the Cotswolds ... all the way from Cornwall. Mum, dad, me, the tools, the luggage ... and my bike, of course!

All thanks to that pre-War MG, without which it would never have happened.

I've had many sports cars of my own since then, many of them MGs. And today I still drive and compete in an MG.

Charles Boulton still at speed today in his fast and immaculately presented racing MGB

THANKS DAD

BY MARK SIMPSON

Mark Simpson is managing editor of *ClassicCarRestorationClub.com* – a terrific club with an online resource of old car news, technical Q&A, tools, articles and even '*How to*' videos where one can see experts such as Mark carry out all aspects of car restoration from electrics to engines and brakes

to upholstery – as if you're sitting with him and he's doing the whole thing step-by-step just for you!

I love Mark's club and I was thrilled when he agreed to contribute a chapter to this book.

My father was not a "car guy", although he grew up on a dairy farm in northern Minnesota, and was no stranger to work. The lessons he taught me, to work hard, self-reliance and to always do the best you can, have served me well. Even though he passed away a few years ago now, my memories of him and the lessons he taught continue to influence me today. As Father's Day approaches I can't help but recall one of the last times he visited me in the shop.

"So, when are you going to finish it?" My father's voice rang out as he entered the garage. I believe I've heard those words nearly as often as, "So, what color are you going to paint it?" and from far too many people to recall. Certainly dad could remember the many times I drove the Chevy over to visit, but the simple fact that the old car was all apart again seemed to cloud his memory of it. I paused for a moment; in the same manner I had for the countless others who asked the same question.

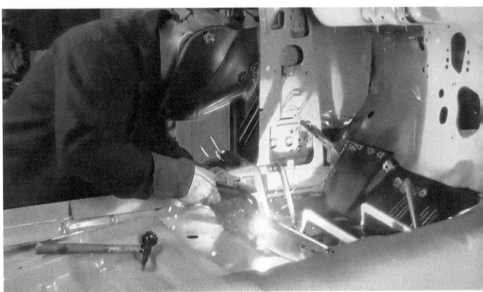

I explained, "Dad, it's not a race to get it done quickly; it's a hobby."

I could tell by the look on his face, as he scratched his head and made his way to the refrigerator for a cold soda, the thought of working on an old car simply for enjoyment was something he never considered. I went on to explain, "Just because it's done, doesn't mean I can't take it apart and make it better." He mumbled something, before coming to rest on the stool next to the workbench.

I grabbed the new driveshaft to mate the 4L60 transmission to the new nine-inch Ford rear axle and slid beneath the old Chevy. As I snaked the driveshaft around the rear axle and through the driveshaft loop, I couldn't help but think how our hobby compares to others. I suspect no one has ever questioned a golfer as to why they have played the same course more than once because it's assumed they want to improve their skills and achieve a better score. Nor does anyone question the fisherman who returns to the same lake, and often the same spot, in pursuit of a bigger fish.

As I slid the U-bolts into the rear axle yoke and called out for a half-inch wrench, it occurred to me that maybe the difference lies in the simple fact that so many consider car repairs to be "work," and certainly nothing about a task that is seen as work could be enjoyable unless it is completed. While the prospect of clubbing plastic balls around someone else's lawn, then chasing after them, only to club them again seems more like work to me, the biggest difference may be how others perceive our chosen hobby.

The distinctive ring of a half-inch Craftsman wrench sliding across the concrete toward my head returned my attention to the task at hand. Dad soon called out again, "I gotta go!" As he turned the knob on the garage door, he stopped to ask, "So, when are you going to finish it?"

I miss you dad, and thanks for everything.

3

NEIL FURBER

"Getting a car through SVA – the 'Special Vehicle Approval' test – is 'Still Very Annoying'"

I first met Neil Furber when he was working for Porsche.

Neil is an obsessive performance car enthusiast with an engineering background operating at the highest levels. It all started for Neil during some passenger laps with Alastair McQueen at Lotus' Hethel test track in Neil's mid-teens. Neil was inspired by the at-the-time chief instructor and

started a journey to understand car handling and car control on a technical level. Like many other car enthusiasts, he spent a large portion of his time honing driving skills and learning to control cars at and beyond the limit.

Whilst still at school, Neil built his first car: a Lotus Seven replica. He started karting with a local club aimed at introducing young people to motorsport and often raced on slicks in the wet. This led to an introduction to drifting around multiple corners on occasions and, although he enjoyed the racing, Neil found the control element more rewarding.

After leaving school, Neil undertook a 5 Year MEng Automotive Engineering course at Loughborough University, including a year in industry at Red Bull Racing. He graduated with a 1st degree Hons and re-joined Red Bull in 2008 to play his part in achieving 4 Double World Championships.

In his private life, Neil is obsessed by performance cars and, although he has spent plenty of time in many different cars, he has only ever owned rear-wheel drive sports cars.

Having built a track-prepared Ginetta G20 and maintained and modified the handling characteristics of two Mazda MX-5s, he has built up a solid understanding of car mechanicals and road-car handling.

As opposed to throwing money and modifications at his cars to improve performance, he has chosen to spend his effort understanding and exploring their performance band to acquire car control that has been described as 'exceptional'.

In the story Neil has kindly chosen to share with us, he describes that despite his experience, getting a car through SVA – the 'Special Vehicle Approval' test – is 'Still Very Annoying'

When Richard asked me for an untold story for this book, the first that sprung to mind concerned the 'process' of undergoing the SVA test to make my home-built Ginetta G20 road legal. For the term *process* I shall say *joy and excitement* but perhaps *pain and suffering* would be more apt!

The original plan was to live at home during my student placement year in order to save enough money to buy the kit of parts plus any extras. Then I'd assemble the car during my holidays the following year at Loughborough University. It would be ready for the next summer. Despite a couple of false starts, this worked quite well and the car was assembled within the year. Then the real 'fun' started. The S.V.A. (Special Vehicle Approval) test examines the whole car in detail to ensure it is suitable for road use. With the correct insurance and a booked appointment you can drive a car to the test if you wish. I now wish I hadn't but hindsight is a wonderful thing! Having built one kit car previously I knew some of the pitfalls of driving to the SVA test. So Dad's Volvo estate was filled with jacks, tools, spare fluids etc.

Attempt one: (Sadly not 'one of one') We were blessed with bright sunshine so we set off very early to do some quick bedding in of the race-spec brake pads *en route* to the Nottingham test centre. (Only one and a half hour's drive away ...) An inspection yielded a particularly warm rear brake so we headed back to the garage to investigate. It turned out that the handbrake cable routing was a little too severe and was causing the cable to bind. A quick re-route got us back on track. Setting off again things looked good. At full road speeds I spotted another issue. The speedometer worked well at low speeds but then wasn't picking up fully to the sixty-or-so mph. We stopped to investigate wiring but found nothing untoward*. The rear brakes were still a little warm so pit-stop jack out, wheels off and the handbrake cable received a further massaged routing.

So with the brakes working beautifully and the speedo added to the list of guaranteed test failures, we set off again. Shortly afterwards the clouds started turning from grey to black. A last-minute dash into a lay-by followed by the Volvo chase car gave just enough time to whip out the cover and protect the car from a short but very heavy downpour.

The post-storm brightening-up gave us some over-enthusiastic optimism so the cover came off and we set off once more. This time we made it to the motorway before the heavens opened again. Stopping wasn't really an option so I decided to just grin and bear it inside my (very necessary) helmet. No windscreen, heavy rain and the spray from plenty of trucks, not to mention the risk of flying stones, there was more than enough justification to choose the helmet over just a pair of glasses!

The further north we drove, the wetter it got. In fact by junction 18 it was getting so bad that I was sitting in a pool of water in my 'bucket' seat. The spray was getting so bad that Dad could barely see my bright orange car even though he was directly behind! My optimism was rapidly becoming strong negativity and a case of all-out physical endurance. It really was bad, I wasn't just being 'wet'.

In fact we never got to Nottingham that day. The engine suddenly lost power, so I quickly dashed off down the slip road at Junction 21 and pulled up on the hard shoulder. The oil pressure warning light came on just as I stopped. Engine off. Hopes and dreams crushed. Upon climbing out, wet and miserable, I saw the Volvo surfing in down what could only be my own oil slick. Opening the bonnet revealed a split oil filter and the mess one might expect to find when high pressure oil has made a swift departure. Luckily I switched off just in time. The oil filter had hit the steering column repeatedly and this caused the failure. Attempt one ended with the return journey on a recovery truck!

Sending the speedometer back to the instrument manufacturer found a faulty circuit board to be the cause of its problems.

Attempt two: One month later, with a shortened oil filter and new speedometer, we tried again. This time I took spare oil and filter too, but more importantly I had drilled two little drain holes in my seat and floor pan. At least now there was a hole in my bucket. Bright sunshine and all looked good. This time we actually made it up there! Of course, it failed the test (due to emissions) but we did make it up there. It was coming home that was not so good! Just fifteen minutes from home we were meandering back

down some local country lanes. The sun was shining, the car felt great, the engine and chassis better than anything else I'd ever driven. Winding it up a little and following a sports car in front, all was going well until mid S-bend something didn't sound right. I dashed into the next side road and switched off. I was met with a strong sound of water draining as I lifted the bonnet. The Volvo swept in behind and Dad's face said it all – again. This time, it was the coolant that decided to escape. I had fitted rubber bungs over the heater hose fittings on the thermostat housing during the build. These were really tight so didn't appear to need hose clips. The extra pressure at the higher revs confirmed that I did indeed need clips.

At least the sun was shining and we were in the corner of a field close to home. Dad likes sunbathing so he stayed and I took the Volvo to get my spare bung and some hose clips from the garage. I had coolant and almost everything else in the car but no bung and clips! Five minutes later we were back in convoy on the way home.

An interim trip to Ginetta found a pair of wires incorrectly mated in the loom to be cause of the emissions issues and it didn't take long to sort. The new shortened oil filter was okay but the spirited S-bend adventure had led to more lateral movement of the engine than before. It had been enough for the steering column to put a gentle dent in the new filter housing. I was back at Uni now so I designed and fabricated an engine stay-bar solution as well as some improved brake reservoir hoses ready for the next trip.

Attempt three: By now we were starting to get pretty good at early starts to build in contingency. I really thought we'd do it this time. The weather thought different! The heavens opened yet again. This time, the engine lost power but it felt like fuel surge – I hadn't brimmed the tank again since the last time. I pulled over on the hard shoulder of the motorway. The Volvo tucked in behind. The engine was struggling to start and felt like fuelling issues so we opted to go and get some petrol and try again. Two plastic tanks purchased and ten litres added to the tank, yet the engine still wouldn't fire. Back on the phone. Recovery truck on its way for the second time. This time, as we waited on the grass in the rain, we had red ants climbing our legs and, since the Ginetta (legally) had no number plates, I even ended up in the back of a Police car for a few minutes while the officer

made a few checks! The problem turned out to be a wet ECU. Some extra waterproofing was added to the list.

Attempt four: This time I wasn't taking any chances. I called in the cavalry and we trailered the car! Finally an easy pass and, ironically, near perfect weather. Finally I could have some number plates made!

So the car was now running well, had number plates and only went out in good weather so the ECU behaved itself. The filter was no longer a worry and all looked good. At least, until the combination of very low ground clearance and crown of the road meant the sump hit a cat's eye! But that is another story ...

Read more about Neil and his life with cars at

www.drive7tenths.com/ramblings/

FIAT 500

BY RICHARD MCCANN

*"Explosions, fires, impacts ... the love affair
with a Fiat 500 did not run smoothly"*

I started trawling the cars for sale classified ads in the local paper in earnest when I was 16. I'd been making a weekly study of these since I was 12 but as my 17th birthday grew ever closer the prospect of actually owning a car of my own became less of an impossible dream.

The small problem of no money, no income and still being at school was dismissed as 'things we'll get over' although I did restrict myself to the more modest cars in the section marked 'Under £250'.

The 1960s Fiat 500 is now regarded as a classic and good examples fetch high prices. But back in the early '70s a roadworthy example would typically sell for £250. Even so, I needed an even better bargain so when I saw a 1965 model in white with grey seats and an MoT advertised nearby for £125 I ran to my father with the newspaper. Could we at least go and view it?

Remarkably, dad agreed and after I called to make an appointment we set off in his Cortina Mk1 Super in search of Italian exotica. Arriving at our

The undeniably pretty diminutive Fiat 500

destination, the car we saw in the driveway was small and a bit rusty. But it was simple and air cooled with 'virtually nothing to go wrong' I reasoned to my father. He was less than impressed, and the brief test drive did nothing to help matters as we both squeezed in the tiny cockpit.

That 500cc air cooled twin engine was fired up by a pull on a lever between the seats which pulled a wire that stretched back under the rubber matting to the rear compartment. There was a choke lever next to it.

Test drive

Dad discovered a gearbox with all the precision of a baseball bat protruding from a bucket of cabbages as he pushed the stick into what he hoped was first gear and with a load of noise and a jump from the 'in or out' clutch we were away. Revs and noise rose as we approached maybe 20 mph, and a fair amount of smoke was blown both out the back and sucked in under the back seat – which is how the 'heater' worked!

I don't suppose we achieved more that 50mph that day, the little half-litre engine sounding strained but I was in love. Father, it has to be said, was less impressed but seeing how keen I was he suggested a round £100 cash to the owner who accepted maybe just a little bit too quickly!

Since I wasn't old enough to drive, dad arranged for the owner to drive the car over to our house and gave him a lift home, and I immediately embarked upon a frenzy of cleaning inside and out. Even our first short drive was enough to show that the little 500 was underpowered so dad set off to give the car what he called 'an Italian tune up' – a flat out drive to clear out the cobwebs.

Blow up

After three or four miles I sensed that dad was starting to like the little car, throwing it into bends and using the gears like a Lancastrian Fangio. As we entered a long straight dad clearly thought he was at Monza and he floored it. 50 mph came up easily, then 60, and we were edging towards 67 mph when there was a bang and the car filled with oil smoke. He killed the engine and coasted to the side of the road.

As we walked around to the back it was obvious that hot oil was dripping from the bonnet cover louvres – not a good sign. Popping the hood revealed a motor drenched in oil, a hot exhaust manifold burning off its oily coating, and a dipstick blown clean out of its tube from excessive crankcase pressure.

Popping the dipstick back in its hole and waiting until the burning oil smoke had cleared, dad fired up the motor again and off we went – a bit slower this time. The Italian tune up had certainly blown out the cobwebs but dad decided that while the car probably needed a new engine, instructing me to simply drive at speeds below 50 mph would be a partial solution, and a more traditional service wouldn't do any harm. So he booked it in to the local garage.

Fire!

Two days later, dad set off to drop in the car at the garage, with me riding along. After less than a mile the car started to misfire, which is a major handicap in a 500 twin. Then smoke started to be drawn from beneath the seat. But this time the oil smoke was mixed with the smell of burning. Dad again killed the engine and opened the engine cover. Boooof! The flames shot out. Dad had decided in his infinite wisdom the night before that a few sheets of newspaper wrapped around the engine would both keep the dampness away from the distributor and serve to mop up all the oil still dripping from ... well, everywhere really. Great idea. Except next day he'd forgotten about the newspaper which has started to burn as the manifold heated up. The addition of lots of air as he opened the hood served to ignite the lot and up it went!

With an impressive display of speed and clear headedness that I'd not seen before, Dad started grabbing handfuls of turf from the verge, ripping them out with his bare hands and hurling them at the blazing engine. It worked – genius. Plus the disaster was caused by the wise one and not his idiot son for once, so I could see many bright spots shining from this apparent disaster.

We walked home and arranged for the car to be towed in, where – incredibly – it merely needed a new set of leads and a fuel pipe to be restored back to running order. I did this work myself with a cheery face and without comment, thus earning myself many team points from the boss.

Dad's Cortina was a sudden gift ...

And that attitude paid off because he subsequently announced that he would be treating himself to a Triumph Dolomite and that I could have his immaculate Cortina. Incredible.

All I now needed to do was to sell the Fiat for what I could get. The burnt paint on the engine cover was sanded down and treated to a coat of Crown household gloss white. I might not approve nowadays, but back then to my 16 year old head it looked almost concours.

That weekend the car was advertised in the local paper, and the first call was from a boy who was a student at the local public school. We arranged to meet and on Monday after school the boy arrived, in a car driven by his chum who had passed his test, and two friends, all in school uniform ... as was I!

... while Dad bought a lovely Triumph Dolomite

Lord Snooty arrives with his pals

The lads were toffs, no doubt about that, and I was impressed. So when they asked to drive the Fiat I willingly agreed, only partly thinking as all four piled into the car that I should have at least asked if the boy interested in the car had a license.

They were gone a long time, and just as I'd decided that they'd either broken down or stolen the car, they appeared around the corner at high speed and under marginal control.

My parent's driveway was marked by two thick oak posts and the young lad sawing at the wheel looked determined while his friends looked terri-fied. A big yank of the wheel in a technique that I'm sure he'd seen Stirling Moss employ at Copse Corner Silverstone was sufficient to break away the rear of the car and for one moment it just sat there, one wheel spinning like a Catherine wheel.

Impact!

Then the tiny tyres bit once more into the tarmac of my parent's cul-de-sac and the car shot forward at full speed, straight up the bank and into the gatepost.

Two boys tumbled from the one door that popped open. Two more were trapped inside but were soon dragged clear. The engine stalled, the dust and smoke cleared and we all stood surveying the mess, the Fiat now resting at a jaunty angle up the bank and with one wing stoved in.

With a demonstration of class that has no doubt carried the idiotic toff into a role today as an MP or Captain of Industry, the boy straightened his school tie, re-buttoned his blazer, pulled himself up to his full 5'4", looked me straight in the eye and, with all the dignity of a disgraced chain store boss facing a Commons Enquiry , said aloofly, "I'll take it."

MORE PRANKS
AND ADVENTURES

BY CHARLES BOULTON

When my friends and I started driving in the late '60s and early '70s, things were what some people would call carefree. Others may say irresponsible, but we all survived and no one got hurt!

For example, when a group of us was away travelling, given a big enough hotel goods lift and a small enough car we wouldn't miss an opportunity to carry a car into the hotel so we could park it outside a bedroom. Then it was the owner's job to get it out again.

On one occasion we discovered a 3-wheel Messerschmitt parked innocently outside our hotel. It was small and light, and only after we'd transported it to the top floor did we realise that it wasn't owned by a member of our group. Oops!

American Motoring Comes to Cheltenham

My first car was something called a Nash Metropolitan. This was built in the UK by Austin but designed in Detroit Michigan and sold under license all over the world for an entire eight year period from 1953 right up until 1961.

It was an extraordinary-looking car, available in a variety of pastel shades presumably to cause a bit of a stir in the drab post-War period.

Nash teamed up with car manufacturers outside the US and let them badge it how they liked. I recall some being called Hudsons. It was certainly a very exotic American car when seen on British roads, that's for sure.

Acceleration to 60 mph was around 22 seconds, and before you laugh, that was almost half the time taken by the VW Beetle which was the Nash's targeted rival in the 'States.

Even when new, the Nash's short wheelbase made it a tricky thing to drive at speed plus it was softly sprung for comfort so it had more than its fair share of roll and wallow on corners.

Sadly my own Nash was not in its prime by the time it came to me. I well recall soon after I bought it that my girlfriend Melanie (now my wife of 46 years) went for a drive into Cheltenham and I stopped at a traffic light that stayed on red for a while. The Nash didn't care to be kept waiting and the boiling water in the system soon discovered a weak point in the radiator hose, which exploded and filled the car with steam!

I walked to a telephone kiosk and called my dear long-suffering father who came out and towed us home behind his Jaguar. Once the car had

The strikingly-styled Nash Metropolitan

cooled down I installed a new hose and refilled it with water, but it was too late – the damage had been done and the cylinder head gasket had blown.

Lacking the facilities to check and rebuild the head or the cash to invest in a machine shop's attention, I simply replaced the gasket, adjusted all the valves and away we went!

This delight in my mechanical prowess didn't last long, however, and within a couple of days the gasket blew again. Another strip down ensued and more checking revealed that things were worse than I feared – the head had warped!

Fifteen-minute 'Rebuild'

Well, the old Nash could forget any chance of a major investment in an engine rebuild. Instead, I resigned myself to a weekly strip down, fitting a new head gasket, and reinstallation. Yes, every week! I didn't even bother gapping the tappets to get the valve clearances right each time – since that normally twice-yearly chore would only last for a week, of course. So I just bolted down the head and near enough was deemed to be good enough.

But it's worth noting that while a job like that would now see the car out of commission in a dealer's service bay for a week, I was very soon able to do the whole job in 15 minutes, such was my familiarity! Incidentally, this isn't a shorthand for 'quite fast', or a case of rose-tinted glasses – I actually timed myself on one occasion and yes, 15 minutes was what I had the whole strip, replace and rebuild procedure down to!

Rapier!

While the Nash afforded me plenty of opportunities to refine my spanner-spinning skills, after a while I inevitably became rather more than a little fed up with this weekly performance, so I sold the car and bought a fabulous Sunbeam Rapier Convertible and drove around all day, looking cool!

When the sun went in I raised the canvas hood and the car suddenly looked less than fabulous – the soft top was absolutely ripped to shreds. A new one was about the same price as the car so – thinking of my father's

Most Rapiers were saloons. Convertibles were a rare and attractive sight

sporting attitude in the MG all those years ago – I simply elected to drive 'roof down' in all weathers!

Knowing that I had no roof on the Sunbeam, one night three friends and I often chose to ride out in one of our group's far less stylish but – it has to be admitted – considerably warmer Ford Popular, always known as a sit-up-and-beg 'Pop'.

The Curious Incident of the Pole in the Night

One time, we completed a great night out where we'd probably enjoyed rather more to drink than was wise. So our poor friend Ray was then required to drive the three of us home. And he was doing a great job keeping the Pop on the straight and narrow as it threaded its way along the dark Gloucestershire lanes late at night while the rest of us sang and played the fool.

It was simply youthful high spirits until one of the back seat passengers (not me!) thought it would be hilarious to put his hands tightly over our driver's eyes just to see what happened.

Predictably, what happened was a crash.

Although we weren't travelling very fast, thank goodness, the car left the road at the very first bend and struck a telegraph pole. That sobered us all up and we clambered out – shaken but miraculously unharmed – to see how things looked.

Sit-up-and-beg Ford Pop came off worst in argument with telegraph pole

The Ford had coped reasonably well with the impact and it was still driveable, and the telegraph pole was still standing upright. So thinking 'no harm done' – except to our poor friend's car, of course – we all piled back in and were rather bad-temperedly chauffeured to our respective parent's houses to sleep the sleep of the just.

Proving just how unfair life can be, the innocent party then drove himself home and parked up outside to let the poor old car recover from its adventure. Early next morning, Ray was rudely awoken by the sound of banging on his parent's front door. It was the Police! We shall never know how they knew it was him, possibly we left the broken number plate at the scene of the crime, but they had traced the owner of the vehicle that had struck the telegraph pole!

'But there was no damage to the pole,' protested our chum. So the police took him to the spot, where the early morning light revealed that while the base of the post was indeed standing proudly upright as we had all remembered it from the night before, the business end at the top of the pole had broken off, with a four foot section including a huge jumble of cables now deposited in the field. A sizeable section of Cheltenham was now without telephones for the day.

I'd like to say that we all chipped in to help pay the fine and damages, but we didn't. And poor old Ray suffered nearly 18 months of weekly deductions from his wages before the debt to the court and the GPO was repaid in full.

Five People and a 10-Man Tent in a Baby Austin

As winter approached, the open top Sunbeam was traded for a tiny Austin A35, which was the saloon version of the Austin Healey Frogeye Sprite that's so popular now. And in another towering example of ignorance is bliss, five of us piled into the tiny car for a camping holiday in Bournemouth!

This was well before the days of camp sites with ready-erected tents – you took your own. So despite the tiny green car and its five passengers we somehow found a way of securing a borrowed ten-man steel framed tent to the Austin!

I'm still not sure how we did it, but we actually made it all the way to Bournemouth. Clearly feeling pretty chuffed with ourselves, we parked up at the camping field and instead of unloading immediately we decided to stretch our poor cramped bodies and ease the suffering of the journey with a quick dash into the pub for a nightcap before we got stuck in to the hard physical work of tent building.

A couple of hours later and 'relaxed' to the point of being utterly sense-less we realised that the tent was still on the car, which we had considerable trouble finding due to a combination of a pitch black night, a howling gale, an unsteadiness of foot and a severe loss of our directional ability.

Fortunately, the other campers – amazingly when I think back on it – took pity on us and made a kind of corral with their cars, circling us and putting on their headlights to provide enough light for us to lift off the incredibly heavy tent and attempt to erect it while falling over in the gale. Next morning we all awoke rather the worse for wear. And then the tent collapsed!

It was a great break though, and we really shouldn't have been surprised when the grossly overloaded little old car ran its big end bearings on the way back home ...

Five people and a huge steel-framed tent surely counts as abuse to this diminutive Austin

Land Rover vs BMW is not a Fair Contest

One more memory for now ... as we moved into the '70s the UK hit a recession and cars were understandably tough to sell. Very expensive and less mainstream cars such as BMWs were particularly badly hit by falling sales, and in an effort to stimulate interest the firm instituted a campaign where you could borrow a brand new car for the weekend to see how you and your family liked it.

The idea was undoubtedly to get people so hooked on the cars that they couldn't bear to give them back and sales would result. Sadly for our local dealer, a farmer near us decided to take the garage up on the loan offer, driving home in a brand spanking new 2500 sports saloon.

One of the 1970's most desirable sports saloons from BMW

Now this was a car that really did cut a dash, intended to sell straight into the Mercedes-Benz and Jaguar top-end sector with something different, exclusive, fast and sporty. Most of us were unlikely to ever own one, they were seriously expensive, and if we knew someone who did own such a fine machine then that in itself was worthy of broadcast. In fact it's amazing to realise how stylish and modern that 40+ year old car still looks today!

Unfortunately for our dealer, the weekend of the farmer's loan coincided with a difficult calving and for some reason that I shall never fully understand the farmer decided to try to transport a calf in the back of the car on that lovely upholstery. It seemed like madness then, and it still seems bonkers now, but that's what he did, presumably thinking that if it was OK in his Land Rover then the BMW would be fine.

Perhaps the car would have cleaned up, or under other circumstances he would have given up attempting to get the animal into the car, so it was simply an unfortunate chain of events that meant his cow chose the very weekend when he arrived home in the new BMW to go into calf.

The farmer saw this as an ideal opportunity – the calf was small so it really would be no problem to transport it goodness who knows where, in the back of the Beemer. Not only was that calf in a state that you really don't need me to describe, but it also relieved itself on the seat and the carpet once the journey was underway.

Come Monday morning and the farmer was as good as his word – the rather less lovely new BMW was returned to the dealership and he explained that while it was a good motor it wasn't quite as practical as his Land Rover. And with that, he retrieved his old car and set off back to the farm.

That BMW never did make it back into the showroom. The dealer told me that all attempts to clean it up and to hide the appalling smell failed. I'm unsure of the car's fate but I presume a trip to a no-reserve auction finally ended that particularly expensive promotion.

CORVETTE!

"Hey buddy – you wanna lift?"

I could hardly hear the man shouting at me above the sound of the Beach Boys at maximum volume from the 8-track player and the mighty 'wuffle' of his 350 cu.in. V8.

I was 12 years old and about a mile into a six mile walk home having missed my bus. In common with most kids of my age, I'd spent the last eight years of my life hearing the message 'Never accept lifts from strangers!'

But surely that warning didn't apply to this stranger. He was young, he was American. And he was DRIVING A BRAND NEW CHEVROLET CORVETTE STINGRAY!

This dude had the lot. Mirrored shades, cool car (one of the very first C3 Mako Sharks no less!) and cool sounds. He pushed open the door from the inside. Of course I got in.

"Where y'goin buddy?"

I told him. "Ok no problem."

And with that, he hit the loud pedal and we were away. I remember that rush of sensations to this day. The sound of the Beach Boys was far too much to talk over, and the driver seemed totally disinterested in me, lying back in the bucket seat, the road reflecting in his sunglasses and the

oh so long hood of the 'vette stretching way out in front of me. I sat low, and the heavily curved fenders protruded either side of the hood. The sensation of power and speed was intoxicating. If I was going to die, this was surely the way to do it.

It seemed like seconds before we entered the little town where I lived, and we weren't slowing down. "Excuse me," I said. Nothing.

"Hello" I shouted. The driver turned to me. "This it?"

"Yes sir. Thank you."

He pulled over and leaned across because I was too flustered to locate the door catch.

I got out, still dazed, not wanting this dream to end.

"So long bud." He tipped his finger to his forehead just like Steve McQueen. And with that, he was gone.

It was a full 40 years before I travelled along that same stretch of road in another Corvette. And this time it was me in the left hand seat. And did it feel as good as it did the first time?

You bet your sweet life it did buddy!

DASHBOARD RETROSPECTIVE

BY JOHN HANSEN

"John Hansen is a great friend and wise adviser from 'across the pond' in Kalamazoo Michigan. A true vehicle enthusiast and a 'proper chap' of the highest order, I'm thrilled to have John's fascinating contribution to this book."

When I was a kid, and a developing car enthusiast, I was fascinated with dashboards. At a car show, the interior of a vehicle was usually the first place I'd go, up on tippy-toes, peering over the driver's side belt-line to have a look inside. I was fascinated with all of the different ways to design a dashboard and integrate all the different instrumentation and features into something useful and visually appealing.

I've never spoken with a vehicle interior designer, but I would imagine that a great deal of thought goes into how a dashboard is designed. Probably more effort than most of us ever consider when we get in a car and turn the key. Let's face it; when you purchase a car, you're committing to look at the dashboard for as long as you own it. You'll likely spend more time looking at the dash than any other part of the car, so they've got to get it right.

Think about all of the different design aspects and characteristics that go into the design of a dashboard. The font of the dash and instrument markings. The size and shape of the gauges and needles. The design, location, size and feel of the different controls and features. How colors and materials are used to create a design aesthetic that makes it appealing to the owner? How can you integrate safety in this design? How do you bring all of the features, controls and instruments together in a way that's intuitive, yet unique, and where controls fall easily to hand? How do you illuminate the dashboard at night in a way that is safe, effective and pleasing to the eye?

As the car has evolved over the past 100 plus years, so then of course have the dashboards that have gone into them. Today, modern automotive dashboards are stacked full of powerful infotainment systems, informative diagnostic and safety systems, and advanced audio and HVAC controls, all with enough computing technology to send Apollo 11 back to the moon, and all in a safe, modern looking contemporary layout.

Obviously, it wasn't always this way.

And so, I thought a dashboard retrospective was called for; a careful examination of some of my favorite dashboards from the 1930s - 70s. I like them all for different reasons. Some are simplistic, while others are modern, elegant and in some cases, perhaps slightly ahead of their time. They all have one common theme – I would appreciate looking at all of them if I had to drive the cars they are attached to.

1930s

1937 Mercedes Benz 540

German luxury at its pre-war finest. Stunning attention to detail and high quality materials. Clear, legible instrumentation laid out in a way that makes good sense. Tasteful application of chrome, and these things are beautiful to look at lit up at night. The 540 was exciting to drive too – with power hydraulic brakes, optional 5 speed transmission and 5.4 liter straight eight with Roots supercharger. 180 horsepower was available to you once you actuated the supercharger by flooring the accelerator pedal.

1935 Duesenberg Model SJ

Unless you are driving a late '70s Trans-Am, an engine turned instrument panel almost assures you a seat at the classy car table, and this dash is no exception. Luckily, Duesey SJ's had the chops to back up the need for full instrumentation to monitor the supercharged 320 horsepower straight-8 engine. For perspective; Ford's flathead V-8 in 1935 made only 85 horsepower.

Honorable Mention: 1937 Cord

More engine turned instrument panels, trimmed with Bakelite switch covers, the Cord was a bit of an oddity in its day. Ahead of its time in many ways, it was one of the first vehicles to offer a radio as standard equipment. It also offered variable speed windshield wipers at a time when not all cars were equipped with wipers at all. Another interesting feature of the car was its pre-selector semi-automatic transmission. That big gauge next to the left of the clock? Oil pressure, which is enormous compared to the radio frequency dial, on the far right next to the generator gauge.

1940s

1949 Jaguar XK 120

This one just makes the cut-roadster production started in '49. Pure simplicity and class; everything you need, and nothing more. Speedo, tach with clock, fuel, oil pressure, water temp, and amps. Stare long enough at the photo and you'll begin to smell the leather.

1949 Buick Roadmaster

Arguably the best looking dash of any GM vehicle in 1949. Simple and subdued, but with classy spun aluminium inserts inside the recessed gauges. Heater controls are to the left of the steering wheel, well out of passenger reach.

Honorable Mention: 1947 DeSoto

Something completely different from the Jaguar and more ornate than the Buick. The 1940s were not a great era for dashboards. The first half of the decade was lost to war production, and the other half was spent scrambling to find out what post-war consumers wanted to look at when they were driving down the road. DeSoto thought you might like the doorknob from your grandma's hallway closet to shift with ... Still, it was an attempt to see what worked and what didn't.

1950s

1954 Mercedes Benz 300SL

How can one look back at the great dashboards of the 1950's and ignore the 300 SL? A technological marvel in many respects, and the first production car to use fuel injection. The dash was ahead of its time- it wouldn't have looked dated in a mid-sixties sports car. Full VDO instrumentation, (and that speedo denoted all the way to 160 for a reason ... in 1955, if your ordered your 300 with the optional 3.25:1 rear end, the car would run out to 160), a fold-away steering wheel for easier entry and exit, and two horn buttons; one on the wheel for the driver, and one for the passenger, underneath the "SL" on the dash left of the cigarette lighter. Mercedes thought of everything.

Triumph TR3

Clean, simple, and in my opinion a better alternative to its closest competition, the MGA. I appreciate how much bigger the tach and speedo
are compared to the MGA, with big, clear printing on the gauge faces. I
like that the ancillary gauges aren't shared like the oil pressure and water
temperature are on the MGA. Another feature offered that wasn't on the
MG- a real glove box. The banjo wheel, the placement of the shifter, just
under the dash, and optional overdrive. There's a lot to like here.

Honorable Mention: Aston Martin DB2/4

Sort of a strange dash before A-M went mainstream with a more conventional dash redesign in the DB4 in 1958. The gauges, up close, are exquisite Smiths pieces, set in beautiful walnut, centered in the dash, with open storage cubbies on each side, a design element later stolen by the golf cart industry. You better have good eyesight if you're going to keep an eye on the water temperature- the gauge sits all the way to the right. It's a mid-fifties dash that harkens back to a bygone era, this would have been advanced in the thirties, but it was old hat in the fifties. Today, it is just classic.

1960s

Mercedes Benz 600

Much like the SL of the 1950s, you can't have a discussion about unique dashboards of the 1960s without talking about the 600. The best everything. Exquisite use of wood- real wood- throughout. It's wrapped beautifully around the gauge cluster, lines the top and front of the dash, and is used all over the doors and trim. Fit and finish to rival many of today's finer cars. This car could be had with any conceivable option you could dream up in the sixties. Phone, TV, refrigerated console, anything you like. Much has already been written about its devastatingly complex hydraulic system which controlled windows, moonroof, seats, and the trunk. A-listers, heads of state, and dictators from the 60s and 70s lined up in droves to get theirs.

Lamborghini Miura

While Enzo Ferrari's company was tearing up racetracks all over the globe in the 1960s, agricultural equipment producer Ferruccio Lamborghini was bringing to market attractive and stylish grand tourers, slowly establishing his company as a force to be reckoned with in the high performance sports car market. Just three years after producing his first car, the 350GT, Lamborghini introduced the stunning Miura. The interior is a leather wrapped, futuristic work of art, and a big change from the traditionally styled 350 and 400 GTs. Note the speedo is as far away from the passenger as possible, probably for good reason.

Honorable Mention: 1963 Corvette Sting Ray

1963 is the first year the Corvette had a dash designed for driving enthusiasts. From '53-'57, the tach was positioned senselessly in the center of
the dash, directly above the gearshift. Things improved somewhat in '58,
when a tiny tach appeared beneath a large half-moon sweeping speedo,
but at least it was finally in front of the driver where it belonged. With
Duntov constantly improving and developing the vehicle beginning in '55,
they finally got it right in '63. The dash was very stylish; you could almost
mistake it as European. Full instrumentation carried over from the '62, but
now the driver gets a huge speedo and tach, and in '63 only, all the gauges
were deeply recessed with what looked like brushed aluminum inserts in
the centers. The gauges lost the silver in '64, and lost the unique cone
shaped recesses in '65. The handle over the glove box made entry and exit
a little easier. The narrow center stack felt like an afterthought to me, as
did the parking brake handle. You can't see it here, but the handle sits to
the right of the steering wheel just below the gauge cluster, and was a part
pulled straight from the Bel-Air. It was a rush job in order to bring the car
to market on-time in '63. In '67, it was properly relocated in front of the
armrest on the center console.

1970s

Ferrari 365 GTB/4 "Daytona"

In my opinion, one of Ferrari's first great dashboards, attached to an equally great car. A terrific improvement over the dash of the 275GTB this car replaced. Full instrumentation with large and clear Veglia instruments. The interior was much more roomy than the 275, however neither the seat nor steering wheel were adjustable. To compensate for this, the pedal pads were adjustable, and could be brought up to 5 centimeters closer to the driver. The gated 5 speed shifter in the pictured car indicates this is an early Daytona. Later Daytona's went with a more conventional, and boring, leather boot over the shifter.

Aston Martin DBS

The DBS V-8 was an amazing car. Smooth, stylish and very fast, it was Aston Martin's answer to its Italian competitors like Maserati, Ferrari and Lamborghini. Upon its introduction in '69 with a newly designed twin-cam V8, the DBS was the world's fastest four seater production car. All the standard creature comforts of a proper GT car are here, and while the traditional Smiths instruments might look a little dated for the era, I think they provide a classic look in this dash. The shifter on the 5 speed ZF gearbox seems like it could have been 2-3" shorter.

Alpine A110

The Alpine A110 is a French built rear engine rally car killer of the late sixties and early seventies. The interior is extremely cramped, but I always appreciated the two oversize Veglia instruments with cut-in gauges for water temperature on the tach and fuel level on the speedo. There is little else to look at on an Alpine dash, and the instrument cluster is arranged tightly, with all important vehicle information clearly displayed to the driver at a moment's notice. Some Alpines lost the clock situated between the tach and speedo, and in its place was a matching oil temperature gauge. The gear shifter is high and close to the steering wheel, great for rally car use. If you ever see an A110 in person, don't dismiss it, as they really are very interesting cars.

Fifty years represented here, and it's interesting to look back on how much dashboards have changed, and reflect on how much more different they are now today. I have some favorites from the '80s and '90s as well, but I'll save those for another day.

Dashboards are great – they help to create a memorable driving experience, and can help you to better understand all that goes on where it matters most; under the hood. The dash provides you with all the vital signs- temperature control, fluid pressure, kinetic energy, all happening just a few feet in front (or behind) of us. Only time will tell how modern dashboards will be regarded- but like these dashboards, and others not mentioned here, I am confident that enthusiasts across the world will continue to appreciate vehicle dashboards that incite excitement every time we slip behind the wheel and watch the tach needle as we blip the throttle or rev match when approaching a tight corner.

Happy Motoring.

John may be contacted at
www.MichiganAIS.com

FERRARI 308 GTS QV

Listen – I was young, OK? I know I was an idiot but let him who is without sin cast the first stone ...

I had finally bought a Ferrari. I'd maybe wasted five years being told by all and sundry that Ferraris were admittedly good to look at but they spent more time in the garage being fixed than on the road and that I really needed a spare car since they were not sensible transport.

And I'd listened. Until one day my boss said to me: "I'm 70 and now have more money than I can ever hope to spend. Family regularly die and leave me their homes. I want for nothing. And do you know what I regret? Never enjoying myself. Never pursing my dreams. Always scared to spend a pound on something deemed not sensible. And here I am now. I could buy a Ferrari if I wanted, and I'm too old and sick to drive it. Learn from me. Live your life today my boy, don't wait for the day that never comes."

I went out and ordered a Ferrari. After all, how many of the 'experts' advising me actually *owned* a Ferrari? None. I'd find that was a recurring theme in later life, in fact. People who had never driven certain cars or ridden certain classic bikes would still lecture me about their failings, even though I happened to own the cars and bikes in question! Nowt so queer as folk eh?

I knew the model I wanted. A 'sensible' V8 not an exotic V12. And a Targa, like the one 'Magnum PI' drove on TV! Red, biscuit trim piped in red, and red carpets piped to match the seats, deep front spoiler, extra aerofoil on the roof above the rear window. This was to be the 32 valve or 'quattrovalvole' model.

I also knew that this would not be a cosseted 'sunny Sunday car'. I did have other daily drivers in fact, including a Light 15 Citroen and a Morris Traveller, but the Ferrari was to be the daily car.

The result? Absolutely no regrets! Driven hard every day, in all weathers, long and hard including a spell commuting to Paris and then in London, the car was perfect. I even used to stick numbers on the car and race it at weekends ...

Dealers told me that a combination of mechanical sympathy (I never went anywhere near second gear until the gearbox oil was hot, for example) perfect maintenance (oh boy was that ever expensive! A service involved engine removal and four cam belts to be replaced at a cost that would have bought me a modest family car every year!) Coupled with regular use this was the perfect recipe for Ferrari ownership.

I'd heard of Ferrari owners being too scared to park their cars without a friend in attendance to protect against vandals or careless parkers. I never bothered, the car worked for me instead of the other way around. And I was rewarded with never so much as a tiny scratch. Admittedly I did let one young man sit behind the wheel once and he managed to tear my leather with a bunch of keys on his belt, but that was my own fault I guess. The cost of the repair by Connolly Hides in London was eye-watering.

The other thing I remember is not really the stuff of book confessions. So I'll make it clear that any high speed work only took place on closed roads and race tracks. Even though we were living in times before Gatso cameras and much less traffic I'd never have done a 160mph run through Kent to catch a ferry very early one morning. Especially since when a truck pulls out doing 40mph the 120mph closing speed differential makes things happen very quickly.

Another thing I'd never have done is to overtake a line of slow moving traffic at 150mph while still accelerating. That would certainly attract the attention of a police car in the far distance, as I believe it did for 'a friend' doing the same thing with a very similar car.

It was getting dark and the friend knew as soon as he saw the blue light in the mirror that he was in trouble, and although the police would never be able to catch him they would certainly call for back up and block the road ahead. Some fast thinking was required.

What he did then was utterly irresponsible and I would never condone such actions. He took the first slip road and turned left at the top, then left again and left again into a housing estate. Then he pulled into the driveway

of what appeared to be an empty house and extinguished his lights and engine. Sirens were wailing on the dual carriageway nearby, and he suspected he could guess why ...

It was then that the friend realised that the house whose driveway he'd parked in was not empty as first thought, since two small boys in dressing gowns and pyjamas had come to the front window and were scrutinising the Ferrari with great interest. He could only imaging the shouts of "Dad! Dad! There's a red Ferrari parked in our drive! Come and see ..."

But no one ever did come and see, and very gingerly our friend restarted the hot V8 and gently – with a sheepish wave to the boys – reversed the car back onto the estate road. Lights on, into first gear and a *very* gentle run home using all the small backroads to avoid the traffic and unwanted attention. If you know what I mean.

That episode, followed by another when a kindly policeman 'let our friend off with a warning' after being timed at 127mph in a racing Bentley had the effect of curing my friend of driving on the public highway at excessive speed, and he now leads a totally law-abiding life. Or so he tells me ...

COSTIN AMIGO

BY GEOFF HUGHES, DEREK WRIGHT PHD

"A 42 year reunion"

Now there're not many owners of a 1970s car who have received international parts and labour support after 42 years. But when we were in Le Mans in July 2014 we were able to help the current owner of Costin Amigo number 3. Granted our support was small – we only supplied a small self-tapper to temporarily repair the boot catch. 'We' in this case are Geoff Hughes and Derek Wright and back in 1970 we owned a small company that produced the bodywork for Frank Costin's company Costin Racing Ltd. Just out of Loughborough University with shiny degrees in Aeronautics and Automotive engineering we'd formed a company making fibreglass items for the climbing fraternity in N. Wales. Having heard that Frank was building cars in the area, we looked up his operations.

©Duckhams BP

73

Finding Frank's factory wasn't exactly easy nor what we expected of a race car setup. We eventually found him located in the small village of Cwm-y-Glo. It was definitely a case of 'don't blink', or you'll miss it'. The only indication we'd found the right location was a small sign above a front window in a somewhat tatty building fronted by a pair of double garage doors that were, once-upon-a-time, painted green.

Walking inside was like, as one imagines it would be entering the pro-verbial Dr Who's, Tardis. An L-shaped workshop went back from the front door and turned right into an area that smelt of sawdust and epoxy wood glue – remember this pre-dates the scrutiny of Health & Safety Executives and fervour of the EU regulators. If the sawdust and glue were not enough to give an HSE Inspector a seizure, the fact that Frank smoked pretty much continuously while he wandered around the workshop would probably have made the Inspector's attack terminal.

During our chat Frank described his aim to produce a long-distance tour-ing car that would have "impeccable" handling. Most of you will know Frank Costin's connection with Marcos and Jem Marsh. Frank's aircraft design

©Duckhams BP

experience gave him the belief that a wooden monocoque chassis could deliver the rigidity and durability combined with the lightness he wanted.

In his workshop, sorry, '*factory*', Frank's four-man team built the chassis and we were able to convince him we were just the guys he needed to produce his body shells in our own newly acquired factory.

When we say 'factory' it was in all honesty a rather large ancient stone-built unused school! Through an organisation called CoSIRA – a quango set up to help develop businesses in North Wales to overcome the unemployment resulting from a devastation of the Slate industry – Merioneth Council had granted us the use of this school building in Manod, Blaenau Ffestiniog. In its favour, cell block 'E' (its basic shape) was big, had high ceilings, a big tarmac playground and a substantial set of double doors which were very convenient for car access. However the massive stone walls and high ceilings weren't ideal when it came to getting temperatures warm enough to cure GRP mouldings. Copious use of polythene sheet for false ceilings, space heaters and with several large electric bar fires we managed – despite the snow that managed to blow into the building from the dove cote style

©Vauxhall Heritage Centre

ventilators fitted to all the roofs of the 'E'. Living and working in the school meant the snow that blew in the roof space settled on our polythene false ceiling above our sleeping accommodation provided a significant test in water flow management as it melted.

Anyway back to the Amigo. Those of you who have read articles about Frank Costin will be aware of his aerodynamic fervour and desire for engineering purity. He was indeed ahead of his time in many ways, and not many of you will realise he was also a fashion leader! Way before the lads of today chose to wear their jeans with the crotch around their knees Frank's trousers were perpetually at half-mast – with a cigarette in one-hand he was always chatting about what was next, while absent mindedly yanking his trousers up with the other. He was always thinking about the next idea but his 150mph brain was stuck with the 30mph zone of commercial reality. This meant that the Amigos we built were all different in some way.

His deal with Vauxhall Motors Ltd meant the Amigo used a 2 litre single overhead cam (as fitted in their Ventora and Viva GT) and the company's front suspension, duly strengthened. Rear suspension was custom designed, based on a rigid axle with parallel trailing links with a 'Panhard' rod for yaw stability. Koni provided the dampers. So, because these fundamental bits and the chassis monocoque were basically fixed, the focus of Frank's stream of ideas became the bodywork. Don't get us wrong, experimenting and changing things were great fun for us but the business sensible concept of keep updates back for Marks 2 and 3 until the sales revenue of Mark 1 kicked-in, just wasn't in Frank's lexicon.

Starting life as an open-top, the original aluminium prototype was soon changed and a roof was added with the characteristic Ferrari Dino 246 style 'B' pillars to improve aerodynamics. This car became the mule which Williams and Pritchard of London used for making the moulds. Other ideas meant that instruments which had started in a central cluster fitted above eye-level to the roof had to be migrated to a more conventional position in a new dashboard.

Further mods saw an engine temperature-sensitive aerofoil inserted into the bonnet's air intake to improve air flow. As the result of an untimely coming together with a Mini on the Llanberis Pass, the combination of the low-slung Amigo and the road's low stone walls convinced Frank that an

©*Vauxhall Heritage Centre*

early warning aid was needed. A pylon topped by a light was attached to the Amigo's roof – so you'll find some cars had this unusual accessory!

Driven, no doubt, by Frank's smoking habit, on one occasion he asked if it would be possible to modify the door moulds so that a self-emptying ash tray system could be fitted. His idea was that by connecting a small chute from the interior door-mounted ash tray to the low-pressure area on the outside lower door/sill the natural suction could eject cigarette ash from the car. We did eventually prevail, having explained that unless he could maintain sufficient air flow (e.g. speeds over about 40mph), mixing hot cigarette butts and flammable GRP resins might not be a good idea! Rather strangely, given Frank's obsession with aerodynamics and his stream of ideas, we could never quite convince him to cover the Lucas headlight cans (as in the E-type and Marcos). In our mind these exposed fittings always looked half-finished.

As readers will recognise, the cynics have always questioned the use of wood in cars. Frank was always keen to take up that argument and meet that challenge. He decided we needed publicity to show the car's capability and durability. Frank managed to convince his backer, the late Paul Pycroft de Ferranti, of the need for greater exposure: Paul agreed and entered a car for the 3-Hour Le Mans.

Some lessons can be learnt the hard-way and experience can be a good school. We didn't need convincing of the car's strength because during a rather spirited drive to our factory, one of the Amigos spun and clipped a stone culvert on the side of the A498 that skirts the waters of Llyn Gwynant. The impact to the front corner at about 70mph ("Honest", Officer) flipped it onto its roof where-upon it slid around 250m. The full race harness-style seatbelts fitted to the cars held the driver in place and he escaped shook up but without any injuries. The front quarter of the car was wrecked but, despite Amigo's impersonation of an inverted speed skater, the roof sustained only deep scratches, and just a corner of the wooden chassis needed major surgery. A new screen, bonnet, a few front suspension components, a little marine ply and some glue soon saw the car painted and as good as new.

Unsurprisingly, the decision to enter the 3-hour Le Mans gave Frank a chance to let his enthusiasm spring forth. He told us he wanted the lightest bodywork possible for his racing Amigo. We were aware that in 1968

©Andrew Duerden

Rolls-Royce had managed to use the extraordinary properties of carbon fibre to produce turbine blades. We hunted down Du Pont and convinced them to sell us a roll of carbon fibre tow for a little under £100 (1970s money, at today prices that's about £5,000!!); bear in mind this was long before carbon-fibre mats and sheets were available. The manufacturer's instructions were brief but very clear – do not handle the fibres as they will be damaged and the resulting abrasion will ruin the filament strength. Since we were about to use the skeins for hand laying the fibres in moulds, this was just our first challenge.

©Dr D Wright

Clearly the carbon fibre was expensive stuff so we needed to use the material efficiently and so we tried to ensure the fibres were laid along the main stress lines of each of the body parts: the photo of the car's bonnet shows it in its natural state. To avoid excess weight no pigment was used, and the carbon fibres were sandwiched between the lightest glass fibre matting on the market. The result was that we managed to get the weight of the bonnet to less than 6kg; compared to the 'standard' bonnet at about 30kg.

©G Hughes

As some of you may know, polyester resins are manufactured by starting a chemical reaction and then stopping it before the resin solidifies. The reaction is kick-started again using a peroxide-based catalyst which causes heat and the resin then cures solid. Here came our second main challenge; the wonderfully thick stone walls of our School meant getting the layup area of our workshop warm enough so the catalyst would work wasn't easy. Heating the building was only part of the challenge as it was also late winter in Wales. Working under these conditions was indeed a 'warm' experience and, combined with the heady fumes of the curing esters, it

©G Hughes

became an almost out-of-this-world experience. You may also remember from school physics that Carbon is an excellent conductor. Light and very fine filaments of carbon would float in the atmosphere until drawn by the convection currents from the exposed elements of the electric heaters, whereupon they exploded as they shorted on contact. Generally these pyrotechnic displays did little more that startle us from our ester-induced stupor as the filaments were so fine they immediately burnt, well before the School's ancient fuse-wires blew.

Producing car bits made from GRP requires the use of moulds and, obviously, once made, the component has to be removed from the mould. Commonly, a release agent is used, but because we didn't want the surfaces of the bodywork contaminated we used a high-grade pure beeswax polish. You can see from the photo and those of the finished car's body shape there were a few complex curves. These curves and the lightweight nature of the race car's body panels proved a further challenge.

The normal road-car panels were thicker and more rigid and would easily withstand the relatively brutal handling sometimes necessary to release the more stubborn areas, such as the bonnet's headlight cans, rear window and front panel. In the case of the race-car, while the carbon fibres provided panel strength, the thin laminate had little inherent rigidity, so extracting the bonnet and the main body-shell was time consuming, and the doors were a particular nightmare. As sub-contractors and because our micro-company would have to stand the cost of replacing any duff panels, the project was just a tad traumatic. A few long days and nights and we were able to get the car assembled and back to Frank's workshop for all the mechanical bits to be added. Compared to the normal road car it was fitted with fully rose-jointed suspension. Power was supplied by a dry-sumped Ford based Hart prepared BDA race engine through a Hewland close ratio box with all the other 'race' required paraphernalia such as the usual Graviner fire protection systems.

The trip down to Le Mans was largely uneventful, although Paul's Bedford transporter's 6mpg meant we needed very frequent stops for petrol. Paul's transporter had previously been owned by Peter Sellers and was equipped with a two tier internal platform. Brian Hart's company had built and provided the ubiquitous Ford twin-cam race engine with Paul and Brian as the nominated drivers for the race.

Scrutineering provided an interesting debate, with the French engineers being both highly sceptical and highly amused, describing the car *une boîte d'allumettes!* Frank, however was not quite so amused by having his car described as having been constructed from matchboxes. After agreeing to cut large holes in the left sill to aid cooling of the exhaust, the car was cleared by the scrutineers.

©G Hughes

The Amigo performed exceptionally well in practice, managing to over-haul the Renault Alpines, several Porsches 911s and more than one or two very loud 7 litre Corvettes completing Practice ahead in its class. The Race started well, but when we came to change the tyres we found the wheels that Firestone had factory-fitted with tyres and delivered direct to the circuit had the wrong hub offset and fouled the front callipers. Frustratingly, by the time we could change the tyres across to the original set of wheels, we had lost too much ground on the competition, and Paul decided to withdraw from the race.

Alongside these activities we had moved the complete operations to Little Staughton airfield near St Neots on the A1. The airfield was owned by Brooklands Aviation Ltd who was in the process of developing it as an industrial/business centre.

In total we'd built some five cars before Paul decided not to finance further production, which was some way short of Frank's aim for a production capability of 150 per annum – but, hey, it's not about quantity but quality, and since the car drove to this year's meet at the Le Mans Classic we must have got most of it right.

We would like to thank BP for permission to us their photographs from the Duckham's magazine. We'd also thank Andrew Duerden of the fascinating Vauxhall Heritage Centre for his hospitality and hunting through his archives at Luton to find photos that filled gaps in our own collection.

©G Hughes

10

ME AND MAXXIMO

"For a racing driver, Neil Furber's relationship with a small minivan takes some explaining ..."

For those who know my background, my short term relationship with Maxximo will come as a surprise. Normally I'm found in race cars or sliding high end sports cars around, yet here I was having just as much fun on a sun-drenched expanse of tarmac in an Indian market minivan. Perhaps a joke of a machine by modern European automotive standards? But was it?

It all started during a work trip training automotive engineers in vehicle evaluation. We had a range of products to compare and contrast. I couldn't understand why they'd bothered to bring this tiny, fairly rubbish vehicle to the private air-field. As the course went on, the engineers started to evaluate the vehicle and kept finding flaws in it – ergonomics, performance, gear change feel. The list goes on. I was sat next to them in the only vehicle with no air-con in the searing heat. Sat on a double bench seat with a single seatbelt across both positions (!) and having heard of a recent roll-over event, I didn't feel all that great. Particularly since I knew the surface was the special high friction tarmac used on airstrips that, it just so happens, helps roll lightweight vehicles with a high centre of gravity during heavy cornering.

But then it was lunch time. We all jumped into the cars to head off the strip and back to the open-air canteen. All the other keys were gone so it was Maxximo, or walk. My two colleagues jumped in and we started heading back, knowing the laughable tiny top speed and 'stir-the-soup' gearbox were going to be a pain. But then it happened. I fell for it. My mind stopped thinking like an engineer and my off-duty side appeared. A couple of quick questions jumped out of our mouths. 'Let's see what it does in the corners?' and 'Since it bogs down even from 2nd to 3rd, can we flat shift?' Suddenly I was back to my 15 year old self hammering round my friend's dad's fields in a beaten-up brush-painted violet mk2 Fiesta 1.1 Popular with no boot lid and not a care in the world.

Speed no longer mattered. Stirring the gearbox and experimenting in a safe, closed environment allowed us to answer those questions and the real character of Maxximo latched onto me. From then on I was smitten

– this cheap, comedy taxi with its Micro-Machines-wheels and questionable safety was now my favourite. I knew the best car was the Honda for all the Japanese engineering reasons but there was no character. No soul. This tin can, its lawn-mower engine with more lag than the biggest turbo I could imagine, and its steady-state rev-limiter had become my friend.

From then on, for every shuttle run, people looked for Maxximo's keys. And every time I'd kept hold of them, not wanting to share my new favourite toy! In the end, the engineers thought the car was very poor, but I wanted to buy one. Just £3k for a brand new van capable of taking my eight friends, my bike and a bbq across the fields for a picnic in the sun. With simple engineering that I knew I could fix in minutes. If only I had a farm and somewhere to run it completely off the UK roads.

After all, I've never come across a car that porpoises so comically as it starts to oversteer!

11

WEEKEND WRESTLING WITH A WRETCHED OCTOPUS

"We all know about those 'little jobs' that somehow turn into epic struggles. Here, race driver, writer and engineer Neil Furber tells us his story ..."

'I've got no heating and it was freezing cold today!' she said. No 'Hello, how was your day?' or 'You'll never guess what happened today!' She was cold and miserable. And rightly so! The ambient temperature was around freezing and a 45 minute commute on the M1 in a car with no heating would make us all a little tetchy!

Sadly I couldn't do anything significant that night in the dark but I did a bit of fault finding around her Mini's heater unit. It seemed to be running low on coolant. The header tank was a little low and there was a gentle dripping when hot and under pressure. The following day I was dispatched to Halfords for some top-up coolant. I made an appointment with my local man and got the car to his garage. To cut a long and shivering story short, a pressure test found the problem to be a cracked weld on the plastic thermostat housing.

Her Mini is no longer that young, and the heat cycling of plastic parts tends to be a little destructive, so this was hardly a surprise. We were now losing approximately one whole litre of coolant a day! My goal was to book it in to the local Mini dealer and get the bits changed. Easy peasy, job done! Sadly not ...

One local dealer had no room at the inn, no courtesy car and apparently no parts/service staff available (or interested!) The next dealer was more helpful but my direct questioning found that the required part was not in stock. In fact, not even in circulation. There was an eight week backlog to supply and get through before we'd even be at the head of the queue for parts! At least I managed to get a new radiator hose to replace the damaged item spotted during the inspection.

So now I was in a quandary. Mini had no parts. We had no time. Thankfully I managed to find an aftermarket item through my friends at Euro Car Parts. The last one on the shelf! Now the only problem was, my local trusted man-with-garage was fully booked. And Mini were not going to fit non-Mini parts even after they would charge £85 for an inspection (that we didn't need).

It turns out that the modern world can be a pretty handy place! A bit of Googling found a very comprehensive video on YouTube. (Funny how brand names are becoming verbs!) One very helpful man had performed exactly this job on an identical engine with a point-of-view camera for the whole job. He even listed the tools needed and showed how all the hidden fixings

and clips worked. After that, confidence built on necessity. My weekend plans were scrapped and the weekend wrestling was booked.

Thermostat housings, in my experience, are normally fairly simple units with two or three hoses meeting the engine. The previous Mini unit was nice and simple. Two hoses and three bolts. This variant can only be described as an octopus. Later dubbed a *wretched octopus*! On top of that, the engine bay of an R56 Mini Cooper S is best described as a rats nest. And the wretched octopus was hidden below the 'roof' of said nest.

The job seemed like 30 mins work in the (truncated!) video. It took a little longer, but I managed to get it all sorted. Within three hours. On the drive. With some time out since rain stopped play in the middle. I even righted a few wrongs with clips and fixings that had been mucked about with during a previous owner's care.

Sadly, modern cars are almost *too* clever and there are sensors upon sensors. The following day was a fault-code-fixing-fest and took longer than the rats nest expedition.

At least, whilst I had all the nest out, I found out why the Mini has such a nice gear-shift feel. But we'll leave that for another day!

12

BLUE TRAIN

"Which Bentley is your favourite? Please don't think I'm boasting, but I have pretty much one of each, so the choice is yours."

This was the voice of Bentley legend and 'Blue Train' car restorer Hugh Harben. He didn't know much about me, so why on earth had he chosen me for this honour?

Where I lived on the Staffordshire/Shropshire border, we were blessed with a few really top drivers. Avril Scott-Moncrieff was a regular at the local

The Bentley as discovered by Hugh

The Blue Train race as imagined by artist Terence Cuneo

supermarket, her Grand Prix Bugatti being parked outside! "Where do you store your luggage when you go on a long trip?" someone asked Avril's husband, Bunty. "We tape our toothbrushes to the handbrake," he replied, with a twinkle in his eye and a twirl of his moustache. A great couple.

So maybe it was via the Scott-Moncrieffs, I'll never know, but Mr Harben later revealed that he had been persuaded to part with his beloved 'Blue Train' Bentley to a young enthusiast for a very low figure to fulfil that chap's dream.

This is the car that Le Mans winner Wolf 'Babe' Barnato drove from Nice all the way to his club in London, racing his friend who took the Blue Train.

The young man (so Hugh told me) immediately entered the car for auction and pocketed the huge sum of money that Hugh *could* have sold it for. This, understandably, left a sour taste in Hugh's mouth and he had withdrawn from helping young enthusiasts ever again.

But there's a bit of an unwritten code that those of us fortunate enough to be custodians of wonderful things need to share them with others, and for a legendary gentleman such as Hugh Harben he just couldn't stop himself sharing the passion.

Accordingly, I was duly invited to his home to take a look at a few of the Bentleys in his collection. There was the 440,000 mile Mk VI special, bodied in 20s style with Hugh's own personal modifications. This is the car that he used daily in his travels to airports around the UK as an aircraft braking specialist.

Apparently, someone once impertinently told Mr Harben that he disapproved of the modifications made to the Bentley. "Well, I discussed them with W.O Bentley and he approved," explained Hugh, politely.

Two legends. Hugh Harben (left) discussed his 'special hybrid' with WO Bentley

Wow. If the impertinent 'expert' had any shame the ground should have swallowed him up there and then. But I guess his misplaced confidence was undented – we all know the type don't we?

Next to the Special was the most amazing original Speed 6 Le Mans car I'd ever seen. "Oh you like that one do you?" said Hugh. "I was asked to take it to a show in Paris in February. I have to tell you that was a cold drive. At one point I was wiring a spanner to the exhaust manifold and then holding it in my gloves, passing it between my hands to keep my fingers moving."

Most people, when faced with such an incredible motor car and a show in Paris would simply call a transport firm and have the car moved to and from Paris in a covered lorry. To Hugh this would have been inconceivable, he had a Le Mans Bentley and a drive to Paris and back in February would be fun! I was with him on that, and I was fortunate enough to do the same trip myself, a few years later ...

Back to that evening at Hugh's though, and he fired up the Speed 6. "Let's go for a drive!"

I marvelled at the car's power and sheer road presence as Hugh expertly piloted his beloved car through the Shropshire lanes. Then he pulled over. "See that railway line over there? A lot like the one in the Terence Cuneo painting of my old car racing the Blue Train don't you think?" said Hugh.

I agreed. "Well, the express train is due soon," he continued, "fancy a drive yourself?"

Me? Drive this car?

With mixed emotions – fear, excitement – I agreed. No way was I going to be rude and decline such a wonderful offer. But similarly, how on earth could I drive this car? And with the famous racing driver owner sitting right beside me.

Thankfully it was all just too much of a rush to think, just as well. Into first gear, up with the heavy clutch, a tiny puff of fuel and that massive mountain of power takes over. Into second, a slight pause in neutral on the way since this is a non-synchro 'crash' box.

I waited for the awful sound of grinding gears and to be asked to stop while Hugh took over and I returned back to his house in silence and shame. It didn't come! We were in second, after possibly the smoothest gear change I've ever made before or since. Thank you God.

Up to third, then fourth. Still perfect. I knew it was impossible but somehow it was happening.

"Well, you drive well enough, my boy," said Hugh. If this was a dream I didn't want to wake up. "Look over your shoulder," said Hugh, "the train is coming. Foot down. We race!"

And there we were. Me. The car. The train. 80 mph on the clock.

Let's leave the story there. My eyes are just a bit blurred as I write this, for obvious reasons. That day was the start of so much. Racing, restorations, good friends, good fun, a spell as team captain, Mille Miglia, Silverstone, Montlhery ...

You gave me all that Hugh. I can never thank you enough but I shall never forget, I promise you.

Post script

There's a moral here, and maybe I'm finally old enough to re-tell it without appearing presumptuous.

The great driver, writer, car-designer, raconteur, film-maker and best friend anyone could ever have, A F Rivers-Fletcher, once told me of a conversation he had with S.C.H. 'Sammy' Davis, journalist and Le Mans winner. Sammy's lifelong love of cars, and indeed his entire career, had been sparked by a chance offer of a ride in a sports car given by its driver as he saw young Sammy admiring the car as he waited to cross the road at the traffic lights one morning.

With my mentor,
Rivers-Fletcher

Sammy never forgot that ride, or the driver's generosity. 'No matter if you don't think you have time,' said Sammy, 'if you see a young enthusiast admire a car you're fortunate enough to drive, you MUST stop and give him some time – and ideally a ride.'

Hugh knew Sammy very well, and I suspect those words were in his head when he made time for me. Those of us with old cars – and I suspect that includes you, dear reader – should follow suit. You never know where it may lead ...

13

DAVE'S CORTINA

Years ago, when we petrolheads had hair and good looks in abundance, what we also had was rust, smoking engines and plenty of breakdowns. On the plus side, unlike today, a few basic tools thrown in the boot were usually enough to get us back on the road again.

I'm delighted to now share the experiences of Dave Girling.

Dave has many years' experience with old bikes and cars, exploring Europe in a Cortina and a Beetle during an age when many of us felt intrepid if we ventured as far as the Norfolk coast!

Dave's Mk1 Cortina is a significant motor. The '50s had given motorists cars with names such as Popular, Prefect, Anglia, Westminster, Oxford and Cambridge. Worthy and a bit dull. Suddenly. Ford offered the swinging '60s a blast of continental style. The Italian name – Cortina! – matched the glamorous styling and people flocked to buy.

Within just a few years, though, youngsters such as Dave (and me!)

could afford a well-used version and what an experience they offered us! Here are Dave's recollections:

One of my girlfriends' fathers had a Morris Oxford. The sills rusted away, so he tacked on rubber car floor mats and sprayed them the correct colour. Who needed MOT's?

The first time we hired a caravan I had loaded the front of the caravan up too much and we were driving home from Cornwall in a Ford Escort estate in a gale. The front of the Escort kept bouncing up, being blown sideways and then coming back down. Very scary. I quickly moved a heavy load from the front of the caravan to the back of the car. It was then perfect but not the best way to learn.

If we are of the same era then you might be interested in my motoring history in case it has any parallels with yours. I know the number plates for most of these.

It starts in 1965 when I was 16 and a mod. In some cases I had 2 vehicles at once. Later motor bikes were as well as cars. Some cars were 2nd cars I had for short periods to do up and sell.

Lambretta TV 175 scooter followed by a Lambretta TV200 (bought new £145).

Then an Austin A35 van – the right suspension failed, it leaned to the right and I could out-corner anything on right hand bends, but very careful round left hand bend! I think the most people I had in it was about 10, no wonder the suspension broke. I had a replacement engine and they sold me one from the 1100 car by mistake. I had to fit an electric pump as the old engine had a mechanical one, but it went well.

In the early 70s I had a Mk1 Ford Cortina 1500 deluxe with bench seats and column gear change. I worked on the engine, fitted 5 ½ J wheels and tyres, uprated the front suspension and fitted an SU carburettor and to me it felt great, despite the ever increasing rust and my increasing expertise with filler. It just made the car lighter and faster as far as I was concerned.

After having a plate welded on for a "wobbly" steering box it passed its MOT and a girlfriend and I were off to Scotland. Driving in Scotland I noticed it started to "dive" in to corners and I thought I saw a wing vibrate, so I took it to a garage in the depths of Scotland and asked him to look at it. After about 30 minutes the owner asked me to step inside. He invited me under the car, it was up on a lift, and said I was to watch. He put a blow torch on a part of the chassis at the front, and it immediately disappeared.

I still remember his words "son you have not got a chassis, you have got an underseal frame around nothing where a chassis used to be. I will weld it up for you, take it home and sell it".

He welded a bar across the bottom of the car and put another across the top between the top of the two front suspension units. It drove home very well, Scotland to London in a day, which in those days was quite an accomplishment. Soon after that the Diff' started to growl, I took it out and tightened it up using best guesses, then later read about all the very careful calculations on how to do it properly. By sheer luck I had adjusted it correctly. Soon after when the engine started to occasionally blow smoke (as cracked rings lined up) I decided enough was enough. I put it in for an MOT so I could say what was wrong with it – and to my amazement it passed. Those were the days!

I advertised it for £40 and two possible buyers came round so I took them out for a test drive together. The diff didn't growl, the engine didn't blow smoke and it drove beautifully. They looked at the wheels, the suspension, the carb' and the new MOT and made similar comments: "At that price it must be stolen", "At that price it must have a lot more wrong with it than you have told us" etc.

I had told them everything including all the metal I had replaced with filler.

So I upped the price to £60 and the next buyer bought the car!

When I had the Cortina I went on holiday in Geneva with a friend and we hired a Beetle. The photo shows me sitting on the Beetle. The other thing I remember about the Cortina is that I

once dropped my girlfriend off at her flat in Central London on a very busy road. The starter motor had come loose and when I tried to start the car to leave the starter caught fire. With cars driving past I had flames under the bonnet and me in the boot trying to untie my water bottle that I carried for the radiator. By the time I had undone it the fire was out. I tightened up the starter motor and it worked perfectly for the rest of the time I had the car.

The Cortina was the only car I have owned that had 3 forward gears, bench seats and a column change and I still remember it with fond memories. Rust and all. Oh ... and the girlfriend is now my wife – I think the car must have impressed her – or not.

When I had the Cortina I went on holiday in Geneva with a friend and we hired a Beetle. This is me sitting on the beetle and then me more recently. The hair and trousers have hardly changed!

As a final note on the Cortina, I do still keep a couple of the parts, not sure why. The Zenith carb was replaced by a twin choke Weber. Not sure why I have the light, I think the 3 lenses are correct.

Other memories ...

- VW beetle (1949 I think. Six volt, small back window but not split back window. Bought for £60 pounds sold for £90 after I worked on it!

- Morris Minor side valve. (It was old and 998cc or 848cc I think but can't remember)

- Honda CD175

- Hillman Avenger

- Mk2 Ford Escort Ghia 1.3

- Mk3 Ford Escort 1.6L estate (This and the Lambretta are the only vehicles I ever bought new)

- Mk2 Ford Granada 2.81 Ghia (bought from main dealer, drove beautifully but had a few strange problems or bits missing that worried me. In a month I took it back to the dealers four times. Years after I sold it the DVLA wrote asking if I knew it was a "cut and shut")

- Ford Sierra 2.0GL (Dealer gave me my money back for the Granada and I bought this).

- Kawasaki Z400

- Ford Mondeo 2.0 Ghia

- Skoda Octavia 1.8 turbo (licence looser if I had kept it, but very nice).

- Honda CBF600R

- Toyota Rav4 2.2 diesel (to beat the potholes)

- Toyota Avensis 2.0 diesel estate (to get the bikes in the back).

The Avensis and bicycles is all I have now. What next, who knows?

14

MORE BENTLEY ADVENTURES

Many years ago, 'Dixie' Dean and the Isle of Man tourist board were working hard to resurrect the car TT, which had, I believe, been held back in the 20s and then kicked out by the world-famous bike TT.

The organiser wanted to pull in the world's best classic and vintage cars and they asked me to put together a team of Bentleys. George Daniels, the legendary watchmaker and President of the Society of Horologists lived on the island and he promised to race the world-famous Birkin Blower, the car that broke the speed record at Brooklands in the 1920s.

So I assembled a team that included collectors John May, Peter Gooch, Michael Steele, Stanley Mann and John Lloyd as well as Spitfire pilot Spencer Flack. Spencer was my dear friend and he tragically died racing the BRM Formula 1 car that I had helped acquire for him. I miss Spencer every day of my life but he lives on with many of us.

Spencer brought along his red 8 litre 150 mph car and kindly offered me his 1927 3/4 ½ which was a 'hot rod' of the type sold in the '30s by WO Bentley's brother HM Bentley, who came up with the idea of taking old 3 litre cars, shortening them and dropping in the more powerful 4½ litre engine to produce the GTi of the day!

The little 4 ½ was a revelation to drive, so fast and with great handling, and I thrilled to come in second behind Spencer's 8 litre. Spencer let me use

George with the Birkin Car

Checking lap times. Messrs L-R Gooch, Zimmer and Flack

that car a lot during the following years, and many people thought it was my own car, such was his generosity. I had a lot of success in it, and I'll never forget my first race with the car at Silverstone. A blue flag means 'warning, faster car approaching you from behind' and it's a signal to maintain your line and let the rocket man come through on his way to a win.

At Silverstone, starting from the back of the grid because it was a handicap race where the faster cars are penalised, I was surprised to see the blue flag. Surely the leaders weren't about to lap me so soon? It was only after a while that I realised all the blue flags I could see up ahead were warning drivers about *me*, approaching at speed from behind them. I'd never experienced racing any car so dominant and that I felt so entirely at one with. We won that race and went on to many more records. Thanks Spencer!

Sadly, when the time came to sell the car, I couldn't quite raise enough money even though Spencer offered it to me at a very special price many tens of thousands of pounds below its true value. It was still a hugely expensive car

and rightly so. It finally sold to Jay Leno and I was a bit disappointed since we had that car so perfectly balanced, that he took out the engine and dripped in an 8 litre which he then proceeded to twin turbocharge. It's on his website video if you want to see it but I suspect it's nowhere nearly as good to drive any more.

The car is now part Jay Leno's TV Collection

I mentioned Stanley Mann earlier. He was a great enthusiast and fine driver, and a true eccentric. Stanley possessed a great ability to rub people up the wrong way, and I suspect he knew this and didn't care since he was charming when it suited him! He was always very kind and generous to me and I admired the good-natured way he accepted often being the butt of practical jokes when we were racing abroad.

For instance, whenever we agreed a time to leave our hotel for dinner we always told Stanley 30 minutes later, in order that he could practice his French on the receptionist, obtaining the address of our destination and then navigating himself to join us!

Similarly, in Germany once, we surrounded his car with some yellow and black tape we had found. The writing on the tape probably said something like 'warning slippery floors' since we had discovered it in the loos, but it was convincing enough to persuade Stanley that his car had been impounded by the eligibility scrutineers for being non-original. Since Stanley was very proud of his car's originality and scornful of others that failed to meet his standards, this was a sure-fire joke and provoked a gratifyingly explosive reaction.

We once persuaded Stanley that the policemen who had been admiring one of our cars were actually issuing a 200 Euro on-the-spot fine and that he needed to cough up 50 Euros to help us pay it. A mark of the man was that he took his wallet out to pay, and I for one felt pretty foolish admitting the joke in the face of such unquestioning generosity. Top bloke, Stanley!

At hotel, IoM. Note some wag has changed sign to 'Welcome to Le Bent Boys

15

JAMES WELBOURNE

"Pioneer Motorists, 'Air Bridges' and to Italy in an Anglia"

In another story within this book, my friend John Hansen tells of visiting an old family home.

I had a similar experience myself when I visited Mr James Whelbourn of Turvey to hear some of the stories of his family's many motoring exploits. Because James's lovely home was my family's home almost 90 years ago!

James's grandfather Fred Aspinall was a pioneer motorist, owning a Q type Swift back in 1924!

Grandpa was clearly generous by lending his cars to other family members – one of the photos showed James's Uncle David with James's Granny in Grandpa's fine Humber in 1948. Uncle David was driving from Ipswich to Mansfield where he was stationed at the RAF base prior to going to Ceylon.

Grandpa (Fred Aspinall) in his 1923 Q Type Swift

Uncle David and Granny en route to Ipswich from Mansfield where he was stationed prior to going to Ceylon in Grandpas car probably Humber circa 1948

James's father saw a lot of action around the world during the War at the wheel of a variety of vehicles, which probably explains his intrepid nature when he returned to Blighty, thinking nothing of setting out to Italy via the Simplon Pass across the Alps in a Ford Anglia or Austria in a 100E at a time when for most people a holiday trip to Hunstanton represented the longest drive of the year!

Southend Airport, boarding air charter plane.

Approaching Hochosterwitz Castle

Starting ascent Hochalpenstrasse

In Austria at Anif-Salzburg, Hotel Friesacher – large converted farm

And while the destinations were sufficiently glamorous enough in themselves, the family went a stage further and actually flew the car across to France on the Channel 'Air Bridge' – a Bristol Freighter aircraft which took vehicles and their wealthy and often famous owners from Southend airport to Marck airport near Calais. The ticket shows the cost as a colossal (for those days) price of £25 in 1961 for two people plus the Ford!

Incidentally, while many readers will know the name Freddie Laker and associate him with his low-cost airline that pre-dated EasyJet and Ryanair by decades, who knew that he was also the man behind the Air Bridge? Thanks to James for that nugget!

James remembers washing that faithful and much-travelled Anglia, and even at the tender age of five years old he recalled the Lucas headlamps – clearly an example of early brand awareness, even if their unreliability did earn the firm the affectionate nickname *'Prince of Darkness'.*

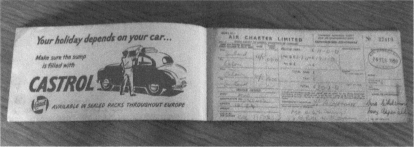

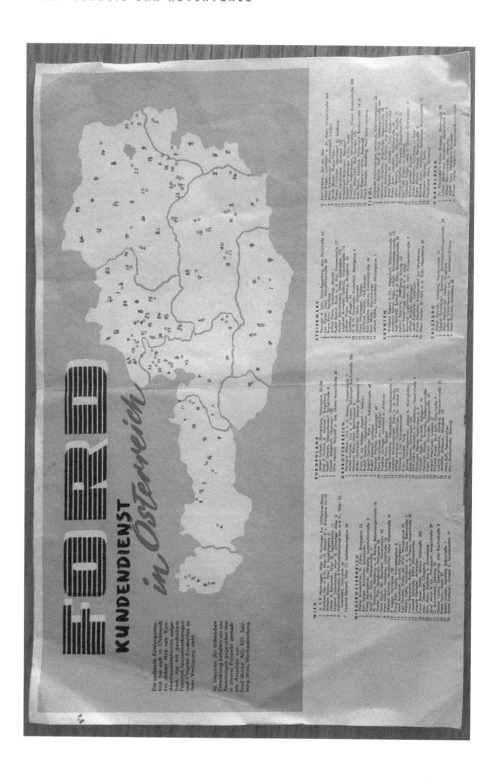

16

MILLE MIGLIA

One year we took the Bentley Team to Italy for the 1000 Miglia. This was a great experience and we repeated the event five times, so I had a pretty fair idea what it was all about in the end! The reason I say that is because it's not a 1000 mile race around Italy any more. Back in the 50s, Stirling Moss won the event by breaking a 100mph AVERAGE speed (ie 150mph + a lot of the time to make up for the village sections) which really cemented the event as the world's great road race.

The sheer danger to spectators means that today the event is a regularity run, with exact check in times at stages being vital, together with adherence to set average speeds along certain sections. Of course, any wrong turn means a flat out sprint to 'catch up the clock' so there's still a thrill as well as lots of timekeeping and navigational complexity to deal with.

One year, HRH Prince Michael of Kent joined our team, and what a great driver he is, as well as being a very pleasant person with a great sense of humour! I'll never forget his catchphrase 'Bumbly bumbly' which he used to describe how he had no intention of going fast; at which point he'd take off, sliding around corners at very high speed, always under full control.

Another year, Spencer and I were drawn no 8. The first day is really odd on the 1000 Miglia. As racers we want to get away, but that doesn't happen

until late at night, for live evening TV and the huge crowds. So the day is spent attending parties and signing on.

Signing on at an event in Italy doesn't involve an order queue like in England, and anyone using the British method will waste a lot of time. It took me a year or two to discover the technique. First of all, check the Italian for your race number. So mine was eight – otto.

Then, at the back of the crowd of drivers waiting to sign on, simply shout as loudly as possible 'OTTO!'

A person at the sign on desk which you can't even see die to the crush will hen reply like an echo 'Otto?' to which you again shout 'SI, OTTO!' and move immediately to the front. People will move to one side since you have obviously been called up. Works like a charm ...

The weather the first day is invariably lovely until evening when it's time to go, at which point it will start to rain and everything – maps, route cards, stopwatches, clothes, you name it, will be soaked. You learn a lot about map covers on the Mille Miglia!

At the start the TV lights are blinding, the roar of the crowd deafening ... and then you're away and it goes dark and quiet as you drive into the night for the first special stage which is usually a driving test – ideal for a cold, wet, tired and confused team!

Being an early number means an early start time. Since that follows a very late night, it's only adrenaline that keeps you going and that's my excuse for firstly navigating the whole team down the 'up' slip road of a motorway at 5.30am (don't call me a pillock lads, you shouldn't have been following me!) and then not realising until we'd got 60 kilometres under our wheels that I needed to turn off at 4k. Oops.

After a lot of detours, we finally spotted Lake Como. Unfortunately we appeared to be on the wrong side of it, but hey, it's still a landmark and you can't have everything can you?

Fortunately, many of the other teams were even worse than us, and after 1000 miles Spencer and I made our final approach at night into historic Brescia for the chequer flag. We were in the lead (but that didn't mean we'd won on timekeeping of course) and for many of that 1000 miles we'd seen an intrepid Italian crew i a tiny Bugatti Type 13 'Brescia' named after the City. If you remember the kids' TV cartoon Whacky Races you might remember Rock and Gravel the cave men in their log car. The sight of the two intrepid Italians squeezed into the tiny Bugatti, smiling through snow, rain, hail (severe enough to cut your face) and scorching sun made me think of the Wacky Races each time I saw them.

Spencer was driving as we entered Brescia and as the big floodlights lit up the road we saw the Bugatti lads right behind us – filthy, cold, soaking wet, but still smiling. I looked at Spencer and he looked at me. It is the greatest honour of the Mille Miglia to take the flag in Brescia. We'd certainly never done it and were never likely to again.

And there, right behind our huge British Bentley, was a Brescia Bugatti, in the Italian city of Brescia, driven by the two Italians. We knew what had to be done. Spencer lifted off the gas and I turned around and pointed to the chaps in the car behind us. Then I gestured for them to come past.

They couldn't believe it. Utterly stunned. I shouted and waved again. Quickly or it will be too late. FORZA! Go for it!

They came past, waving to us frantically, and – to absolute pandemonium from the huge crowd, the Italians in the Bugatti Brescia took the flag in Brescia at the finish of the greatest road race of them all.

We came in first loser, grinning like Cheshire cats. I couldn't speak. 'You're too soft by half,' said Spencer to me, looking soft himself.

"What does it feel like?" said the reporter, in English, as they stuck TV cameras in our faces. And with the great understatement that made Spencer the legend he was, he replied in his mockney accent:

"It's something to do, innit?"

The Italian Brescia drivers, meanwhile, didn't care who thought them overly sentimental. They abandoned their car and dragged us out of the Bentley, crying and hugging us.

I think they appreciated our little gesture.

MORE MGS AND MORE SPINS!

"First I saw the grass. Then the track. Then the marshalls'
post. Then more grass. More track. The sky. And then
a glimpse of the crowd whizzing past my window ..."

It set me wondering if there's a moment in time when a driver's access to fast cars finally exceeds his ability.

After all, I was only in the MG B due to my inability to keep my own MG A in a straight line ...

It started like this.

They say it's crazy to ever go back to your first love. It can never be the same. Well, I proved that wrong. You see, I was in my early 20s when I was introduced to the delights of a stripped out and immaculately prepared MGA racing car.

To be honest, while I'd always liked the car's looks I never paid much attention to an MGA. It's not a V8, after all! Then I drove one. Admittedly the best example of the breed, but still reasonably standard. What a revelation! You sit down low inside, almost wearing it. And the handling ... so responsive, so forgiving. Put the tail anywhere you want, steer on the throttle, there's time to think, to plan. Nothing snaps round to bite you, the car feels like all good race cars – like an extension of your body. It's hard to describe but you know when it happens. Pure bliss.

Well, silly me I moved on to bigger cars, bigger engines, faster, twitchier, less forgiving. Rear engine F1 cars of the '60s that would exit the track backwards in a spin of you were silly enough to lift mid corner. Front-engined monsters with terminal understeer, you name it.

Then one day a lovely chap came to view a collection of Cooper FJ single seater parts I had for sale. He had a lot of cars and rather less cash – like many of us – but he did have a fabulous race/sprint MGA. We did a deal and I'd gone back home to my first love.

The revelation was that it was exactly as I remembered them – bliss. We soon started racing together, and notching up a few wins. Inevitably, the quest for more speed resulted in the 1600 cc engine being swapped for an 1800. This is widely said to be a simple 'lift out and drop in' job. Yeah, right.

Loads of mods later and I wouldn't have bothered if I'd known, but there we were. It worked, more speed, more wins, but in handicap races of course you're penalised so it's pointless! Then I fitted a Tran-X LSD since the extra power was lifting a wheel and losing speed at places such as the Brooklands complex at Silverstone.

The Tran-X was mighty although it made a noise as if a helicopter was landing in the boot! The first time I went out at Silverstone I wondered what the heck was happening – even with my helmet on and the engine and gearbox noise the diff was screaming. Of course, I rapidly learned that this was the sound to look for, and ever wilder slides resulted, along with a couple more 'pots' for podium finishes.

*Richard at Silverstone with MG Legend
Count Giovanni 'Johnny' Lurani*

*Two Heroes: Tony Lanfranchi
and Gerry Marshall*

It was at this point that I decided I'd try going back to hillclimbs and sprints. I'd been reasonably successful at this specialised branch of motorsport a decade or so earlier and I remembered the relaxed afternoons chatting with fellow racers over paddock picnics with particular fondness. Hillclimbs, for the uninitiated, are not blasts up muddy hills. Lots of folk think that, reasonably enough. So just to be awkward, the muddy jobs are called 'trials'.

A hillclimb or sprint is essentially a race track where you (usually) only do one lap or a part of a lap. The clock starts when you leave the line and stops when you cross the finish line. Your time is measured in hundredths of a second and since you start at intervals – like the Isle of Man TT – there's no one to blame for getting in your way so a circuit racer's best excuse has just been lost!

The other factor with hillclimbs is that the roads are often pretty narrow – much more than a circuit. So my hooligan love of power sliding was a positive disadvantage. Accuracy and fast tidy driving with pin sharp corner approaches and exits were the marks of a champion. All the things I'd never bothered about.

'Lurid' was how my first win was described by the commentator, and the public watched me more in amazement how this lunatic somehow didn't crash rather than for any admiration of my 'style'.

Of course, when you're going sideways you're wasting time not going forwards, so I either needed to learn how to drive better or I needed more power. Inevitably, I opted for more power and bought a supercharger!

Now we were really cooking. It had everything – the under-bonnet wow factor, the noise, the power. Of course, we were now probably comfortably exceeding 200 bhp in a car originally designed for 72 bhp so it was getting a bit busy in there.

You just know where this is going don't you? I had a win and my handicap was reduced again. In order to claw back an advantage I bought a set of extra-soft qualifying tyres that while road-legal were essentially slicks with a few grooves cut in them. They came with a warning that they only worked properly when they were both hot and dry.

Getting tyres hot is no problem on a circuit; the warm up or 'assembly' lap does that just fine, and a sensible first racing lap soon has the tyres feeling like they're made from glue. However, a hillclimb is fast and short. The tyres might be warm as you cross the finish line, but they're cold when you start.

Nevertheless, on my first dry warm day with the tyres it went like a rocket. Next day was wet. "Be careful through the first three turns," said a fellow competitor who'd had his first run. "Very greasy."

Early morning paddock

There's often a bit of 'kiddums' in racing, where people say things to make you ease off just a fraction, but this chap I trusted. So when my time came to go I was just a little bit more careful than usual in those first turns. Not a problem, the car felt just fine.

Thinking that the track has maybe dried a bit I decided to let it rip at that point, especially as the next section was what I'd call a wiggly straight. You get the picture? Try to straighten out the curves as much as possible and just blast it.

The first wiggle provoked a slide. I opposite locked and caught it. Maybe a slight over-correction, who knows, but the second wiggle saw us fish-tailing the other way. I caught that slide too. Was this the great Maestro John Surtees behind the wheel I thought?

The question was answered immediately and emphatically in the negative. The third slide was most definitely not caught. The back came right around and I slammed into the Armco barrier at speed, injuring my knees (yet again) and breaking a few ribs. Ouch.

That was the end of my season. Maybe my career, I thought. Amazingly, one competitor and the Sports Car Drivers' Representative in the Championship himself – Mr Charles Boulton, who tells his own story elsewhere in this book – decided otherwise.

The 'phone rang the week after the crash. "How's the Car?" asked Charles. "The damage is pretty cosmetic, MGs are tough as you know," I said, "But even ace restorer Terry Cox can't get the thing fixed and painted for next week."

"No problem old boy," said Charles, "you can share my MGB for the next meeting."

This incredible generosity – and trust with his beautiful race car – was humbling and I was determined to show everyone that I could be trusted in the B. So when the day of the race dawned I was extremely careful in my first practice run. Even so, the power and smoothness of the engine in Charles's car was a revelation to me. Fantastic!

Second practice and I was a little faster but still VERY careful. 'Just happy to be here' was my motto and I made sure that he knew it.

So it's a bit of a pity that it all went wrong for the first race run. A bit of 'red mist' at being allowed to drive this rocket ship saw me flying under the

Bridge at Prescott at great speed and I knew that I needed to stop the car from drifting too far right on the left hander, so I pulled her well in for a lovely tight line.

Prescott

Unfortunately – unlike the A which would have been sliding to the right by this point and needed plenty of muscle on the tiller – the B reacted without fuss to my steering input and we just clipped the grass with the left rear tyre. At high speed and loaded way over into the turn, that is something we call 'A Very Bad Thing'. I've seen people barrel roll out of there after similar mistakes so I felt an immediate pain in my wallet. This was going to get expensive.

A racer never gives up no matter how hopeless it looks, you just keep fighting, so as we spun I corrected. Nothing good happened that I could detect, the view out of the windows as I was flung around was a bit like a turbo-charged merry go round that's had the speed limiter disconnected.

The second 360 degree spin was as dramatic as the first, grass and mud being churned up and thrown into the air, the crowd stepping back out of the way of the inevitable barrel roll.

By the time (only the blink of an eye but it seems like a lifetime) the third 360 degree spin came along I was still sawing away at the wheel with the same lack of style that the great driver Tony Lanfranchi said, when he saw it at Brands Hatch decades earlier, would result in a nest of tables if there was any wood around. But this time – amazingly, it worked!

As the nose of the car spun around yet again towards the direction of the track I popped the transmission into first gear and let up the clutch, re-joining the track without stopping and continuing at race speed to the finish. The crowd cheered and even the marshals applauded. What they chose to overlook was both the fact that the lack of skill that brought on the triple spin far exceeded the bit of luck that got me out of it, and the fact that I raced on was not down to bravado – I simply didn't want to stop, get out and see everyone laughing!

My Tutor – Tony Lanfranchi

My time, I seem to recall, was about eight seconds slower than the practice run earlier, so when I returned to the paddock, Charles, who hadn't seen the 'incident' but had heard the 'time' praised me for going nice and steady in his pride and joy. I blushed but said nothing.

Unfortunately, Charles's second pride and joy – his wife Mel – has seen everything, and now returned to the paddock to give everyone a blow-by-blow (or maybe I mean spin-by-spin) account of what I'd done.

Charles walked slowly around his formerly gleaming white car. It was covered in mud.

"Well, you can clean that lot off for a start!" he said to me, smiling. What a toff, eh?

18

THE MINISTER FROM MONTANA

BY JOHN HANSEN

"Here's another great recollection from John Hansen ..."

For those of us who ride motorcycles, one of the things you realize after many years of riding and owing a variety of bikes are that the imprints motorcycles leave with us after we sell them are not always the same. Some bikes are more memorable than others; sometimes the people we encounter, and the memories we make as the world unrolls before us on the saddle are memories that last.

I had purchased a 1990 Honda VFR750 from a collector in Grand Rapids. The bike, red with spotless white rims, was sold to me in mint condition, practically as-new, with a shop manual and pages and pages of service and maintenance documentation that went all the way back to when the bike was purchased.

A true "no stories, no excuses" bike, with about 13,000 miles on the clock. Having recently sold my SV650, I was in the market for a sport-touring bike that would hopefully not embarrass me too much at an occasional open track night. With its solid single-sided swing arm and silky smooth V-4 with gear driven cams and about 105bhp on tap, the bike was a capable performer, yet very comfortable, even by modern day standards.

I loved that bike. I've owned eight motorcycles at various points in my life, and the VFR is still my favorite. It carried me safely on trips all over my home state of Michigan. I had two great seasons riding the bike, and many adventures with it. I had bought the bike with the intention of "running the wheels off it", and I did.

The first summer I had it, I used it to travel all over the state to visit with relatives, as I was exploring the genealogy and history of my family on my father's side. I made trips to Traverse City, Clare, Mt. Pleasant, Greenville and multiple trips to the village of Gowen to research in the archives of the Little Denmark Church (now Settlement Lutheran Church). The research was fascinating, though I had to learn how to read a little Danish to translate the records in the archives.

While I was in Gowen, I headed north a few miles and stopped at my great-great grandfather's farmhouse in the tiny village of Trufant. My great-great grandfather, Hans Peter and his wife Dortea had immigrated to this area from Denmark in the 1870s. The house, which is still standing today, was built in 1896 after the original farmhouse they had built had burned down. The house was owned by my family through the 1970s.

The couple who own the house today were remarkably kind and invited me in for a tour, showing me several photos of my ancestors that they had found in the attic when they moved in. The farmhouse was quite large for its time, and the current owners have done a great job maintaining it.

While I was there, the gentleman asked me to follow him outside. We walked about 50 yards behind the house under tall trees until we came out to a clearing of farmland. A really big clearing. "Look around", he said "all this land was once Hansen farmland. You can't see it all from here; the farm slowly grew as your family added acres and acres through the years."

It was true; I knew that several hundred acres of farmland had been slowly liquidated after my great grandfather, Jay, passed in 1973. On the way back to the house we walked past what remained of a sealed well, and a subtle chill went through me.

My great-uncle Walter had tragically fallen in that well and drowned in 1887. Walter was 5 years old. I had found the newspaper article about the accident in the microfiche newspaper archives at the Greenville Library. The farmhouse had a large wrap-around porch, and the owners insisted I "walk the porch" as my ancestors had done and they took a photo of me doing it.

My family, on the porch, 1909

I am the only fifth generation Hansen in my family to have done so.

But back to Hondas ...

I took other memorable trips on the bike as well, including a couple of blasts to the Upper Peninsula, journeying across the Mackinac Bridge, with a ferry ride over once to explore Drummond Island. A couple of trips up north just to ride M-22 and see

The Hansen Farmhouse today

the tunnel of trees on M-119, and miles and miles in between those trips for work in and around the Kalamazoo area.

It seemed as though I was always taking the long way home, just to put in a few more miles of fun every time I rode it. Almost immediately after purchasing the bike I outfitted it with a tank bag, saddle bags and a tail bag; more than enough storage for occasional overnight trips. The bike was also a reasonably competent and stable track bike, and saw a couple of track nights at Grattan and Gingerman.

So why sell it?

The truth is I didn't really want to, but I noticed after the birth of my second child that I was not riding the bike nearly as much as I used to. A couple of close calls, one on M-22 and one at Gingerman helped me see that killing yourself on a motorcycle while you have a newborn at home is one of the more selfish ways to bring tragedy to a young family.

So, the bike mostly sat, under a cover in my garage, and that third season I owned it I got it out maybe once a month. In the two preceding years I had put over 12,000 miles on the bike, and the third year I had only ridden it about 500 miles.

It bothered me sitting there. When I was riding it regularly, I was maintaining it meticulously; cleaning it all the time and immediately tending to everything that it needed as the miles wore on. I had even made arrangements to park the bike in a warehouse across the street from my office on days I rode the bike to work to keep the 23 year old plastic and original paint from baking in the sun all day as I rode it to work as often as I could.

A decision point was coming; sell or ride. So late that summer I half-heartedly placed an ad on Craigslist with a link to a YouTube video I had shot of the bike. I priced it at the upper end, as it was still in amazing shape.

I heard nothing for about a month, and as it was headed into the Fall I was thinking the bike was going to go into storage for the winter after all. Maybe I didn't want to sell anyway ...

Then one afternoon in early September my phone rang. The caller asked if I still had the Honda for sale. I said that I still had it, but was considering keeping it. We talked about the bike for a few minutes and I learned that the caller was from Montana. He had watched the video of the bike and was adamant that this was the bike he wanted, as he had bought a red VFR 750 new in 1990 and sold it after a few years. In a fit of nostalgia, he wanted another VFR and was scouring the country for the nicest one he could find. Would I be willing to hold the bike until he could fly in to Michigan to pick it up and ride home?

"No problem" was my reply, but I insisted he bring cash or mail me a check that would clear my bank before he took delivery. He said he would bring cash, and for my full asking price. He said he would make travel arrangements and let me know when he was coming.

Truth be told, I was a little sceptical at the time, I didn't really believe this deal was going to happen. A week went by with no contact, I didn't think much of it, and then I got another call ... He had his plane ticket; in three days he would be flying to Grand Rapids, renting a car and driving south to Kalamazoo to pick up the bike.

We made arrangements to meet at the airport in Kalamazoo where he could drop off his rental car and ride out. That night, I went out into the garage to uncover the bike and get it ready to be picked up. When I took the cover off, I noticed a little oil on the ground under the left front fork. Leaky seal. A visit to the Honda dealer the next day scored me the necessary fork seals and the night before the bike was to be picked up my brother and I dismantled the forks and replaced the seals on both sides. Forks reassembled, air bled, and leak free, the bike was ready to go. I was supposed to meet the buyer at the airport around 6 PM the next night.

A flight delay in Minneapolis caused him to not get to Kalamazoo until nearly midnight. He came walking up in the dimly lit parking lot carrying a helmet, wearing leather boots, jeans, a riding jacket and a backpack. He had long dark hair and a scruffy beard. As he approached, several things occurred to me at once – I was meeting a stranger alone, (I had dropped off my car at the airport earlier that day so I could drive back home) this was a Craigslist deal, it was the middle of the night, and I was supposed to walk away from this with several thousand dollars cash. The guy walked right past the bike and eagerly shook my hand, introducing himself with a smile. He seemed in a hurry, and almost immediately after shaking my hand pulled a big wad of cash out of his pocket. I tried to slow things down a little.

"Why don't you have a look at the bike first" I said. I had brought along a flashlight for him to use, but he passed on that and walked a quick lap around the bike, not bothering to hear it run. "Looks great, man, this is just what I've been looking for!" Again, he pulled out the money.

We sat on a bench in the parking lot while we inked the deal. I filled out the title to complete the sale and he handed over the money for me to count. I had thought to bring a counterfeit ink pen to check the bills with and checked several of them with no issue. With the money counted and tucked away, we exchanged the paperwork and I walked over to the bike with him, asking what his plan was.

He planned on riding to Chicago that night and finding a hotel. From there, he was going to make his way across Iowa, South Dakota and Wyoming. He was planning to meet up with his son at Yellowstone National Park and spend a couple days riding around the park with him on his way back to his home in Butte.

I asked what he did in Butte and he said he was a minister of a small church there, and a roofer on the side as well. We spent a few more minutes in pleasant conversation talking motorcycles, family and careers. With that, he climbed on the bike, we shook hands, and I watched him ride off into the night, off on adventures, making memories of his own, on one amazing bike.

Standing there in the middle of a cool September night, my faith in the decency of humanity momentarily reaffirmed, a thought came to me- until it's proven to me otherwise, I'll continue to believe the tagline coined by the company in the early sixties- "You meet the nicest people on a Honda."

Happy Motoring.

19

A BENTLEY 'SPECIAL'
AND A SPECIAL BENTLEY

"It's up for auction today if you want it."

That 'phone call from Mr Soul set off a panic that would develop into a life-long passion.

Scroll back a couple of years and I was living in a small Buckinghamshire town. The local multi-millionaire had a fine stable of vintage and classic cars, but – as a young man – I ignored the coachbuilt Rolls-Royces and 'brass age' machinery and focussed on a racy looking old Bentley roadster.

The car was often parked in the wide Georgian High Street outside the millionaire's imposing mansion, and I always stopped to look. One day the great man himself exited his house and walked towards the Bentley. I'd known him from my schooldays and he kindly started chatting to me about the car. "It needs using really," he said. "I hardly drive it these days. You can have it for a while to give it a bit of exercise if you like."

Was I dreaming? It seemed likely, but just in case this was really happening I gave it a shot. We have many wonderful inventions in the world but to the best of my knowledge a machine has yet to be invented that's

capable of recording the fraction of a second it took me to say 'yes' to the extremely generous offer and we arranged a time later in the week when I could collect the Bentley.

In fairness to the Bentley's owner, I should probably say at this point that I did have a reasonable car collection of my own at this point, including a lovely 1934 Lagonda Rapide, so he wasn't being silly and entrusting his Bentley to someone with no experience of old cars.

I also mean no criticism of either the car or the offer when I say that the Bentley did indeed need using. It ran badly, steered badly, rode badly ... but it looked cool and my God did it fly! Despite the badly-adjusted carbs and a misfire it still had almost 4 ½ litres of motor beneath that long louvered bonnet and the car was stripped out down to the essentials.

What was it? Well, after WW2 Bentley and R-R – in common with other car makers – were deprived of good steel. Bentley's Mk VI was a 'baby' Bentley for a modern age and sold pretty well. It rusted well too, and by the '60s there were plenty of cheap ones about. And beneath the ailing tinware was a fabulous chassis, engine and gearbox. Tear off the body and – unlike the next generation of unitary construction cars where the integrity of the whole machine is in the body – one revealed the basis of a sports car!

One visionary called Harry Rose, a famous and respected vintage Bentley racer, restorer and collector designed and made some lightweight bodies which he then attached to shortened chassis. As a youngster I recall a London dealer called *Jamie* Bond (yes I think James Bond was really his name) advertising them, and this is the car I had been privileged to drive.

When I returned the car I implored the owner to let me have first refusal if he ever considered selling it, but he said he doubted he'd ever part with it. I didn't blame him.

Fast forward two years and Mr Soul had changed his mind. He explained that he knew that the car needed some work and thought a public auction was the best way to dispose of it. It was only on the morning of the sale that he kindly remembered his promise to me.

Ok we can still do this. Where was the sale? Hampshire! I was a couple of hundred miles away in Staffordshire. Nightmare!

A quick call to work to beg a day's leave and I was in the car and away, screaming into the auction with minutes to spare. There was the car, surrounded by interested parties. No way was I going to be able to buy this ...

Half a dozen cars took their turn to drive onto the stage where they attracted soaring bids, hammer fell, drive away. Now the Bentley's turn. I'm ready ...

Enter the Bentley, being pushed by three men. Much laughter from the crowd. "It's fine," said the auctioneer, "It's just run out of petrol."

"Yeah right ..." muttered a couple of chaps next to me, sniggering. "That's what they always say."

"Now ladies and gentlemen," said the auctioneer. "I first need to advise you that this car's MoT has expired. It hasn't failed, but the owner forgot to renew it. But we are told that it is roadworthy and will probably will pass again f presented for inspection."

Cue for total hilarity from the assembled crowd. Suddenly that were looking not at a lovely sports Bentley but an old banger with no MoT and it wouldn't even run sufficiently to drag itself onto the auction stage.

"Who will start me?" said the auctioneer. No one fancied the prospect. Bentleys are notoriously expensive to repair and who knew what was wrong with this one. One could throw thousands of pounds at a problem car and still not sort it. Only the gamblers in the audience tried a few low bids. So I risked it with a bid of my own. About half what I intended to bid to but why not?

"Any more bids? No? Come along now, it's a Bentley! Come on, fair warning ... no? Going once ... twice ... last time ... any more bids? No? Really? Last chance ..."

The hammer dropped. It was mine!

Sequel

I filled the car with petrol. It started and ran fine.

I took it to the MoT station and it passed.

I then spent all the money I'd saved (plus a load more I admit) restoring the car. What a great machine it was. Tail out, opposite lock everywhere, fast, forgiving, fun.

I eventually sold the car to a charming Austrian aristocrat whose uncle had been the engineer Dr Robert Eberan von Eberhorst who designed the Auto Union Type D Grand Prix car before going to ERA in Dunstable

England for the Jowett Jupiter chassis project, and then Aston Martin to design the DB3! When he arrived to collect the car he had his glamourous Italian girlfriend with him. She'd apparently been promised a ride in a Bentley convertible, and her face when she saw my stripped-out little racer was a picture. She explained that she'd been expecting something rather different.

The guy grabbed her Vuitton luggage and tied it to the fuel tank with ribbons. Then in they jumped.

"Where are you off to?" I asked, presuming he'd say London.

"To my house in Vienna," he shouted. "Where's the M1 motorway from here?"

"Turn right at the end of the road"

"Ok, got it. Bye"

And he jumped in and drove away at speed, turning *left* at the end of the road! He called me a day or two later. They'd detoured through Italy and were now safely in Vienna. A great gentleman, with a great girlfriend, and driving a great car.

20

FAREWELL TO A FRIEND

"Don Homuth says goodbye to his 1978 Datsun 280Z"

At speed at Portland International Raceway, with my wife in the passenger seat.
We are doing about 75 mph into turn 1. Photos by or courtesy of author

Well, old friend, it's time. After 39 years of genuine pleasure at being your owner/driver, your story will now continue with someone else. I've managed to find someone who will re-do and upgrade you to a different level.

The earliest surviving photos I have – before the second re-do

He will keep you with the same or even better level of care than I have. Says you will get a leather interior, a wool headliner, and be kept in a climate-controlled garage. You deserve that.

But I smile when I remember seeing you that first day, and thinking that the Black Pearl paint was so much more elegant than the metallic bronze of my own car. You did have a lot of strange vinyl stripes, but a hair dryer took those off easily enough.

I smile when I remember how I hid you in a basement parking lot at my office till I got the other Z sold. My first wife would not have understood my having two 280Zs simultaneously. But there were other issues than just you.

I smile when I remember how I told friends that I'd still own you in 25 years. Mostly they just laughed. Little did they realize ...

And I smile when I remember all great drives we took together, mostly in Minnesota and North Dakota, during good weather and bad. You were always dependable and a genuine joy to drive. Seeing that long hood out front as the miles went by still evokes great memories.

Powder-coated suspension components

I remember the first conversation I ever had with my current wife was about you. She thought I was kind of a jerk at the time, but I had that "really nice car" ... So I got a second chance. Thank you for that.

She learned to drive a manual transmission in you. She thanks you too.

We thought about selling you several times, but then we'd take a short road trip and then figure that maybe we could wait a while yet. That went on for more than 20 years. Not bad!

After the first re-do in 1987, the last road trip I ever took with my mom, going to visit her old haunts in western Ontario. Her far-flung distant relatives saw you, and figured I was wealthy because I drove such an exotic car. Little did they know ...

I smile when I remember driving out to Oregon in 1987 with a large jade plant (named Fred) seat-belted in the passenger seat. For some strange reason, every pickup truck on the road took a run at you just to prove ... something.

And I remember the second re-do in 2006, getting rid of that 'never to be sufficiently damned' sunroof, replacing all of the rust with metal and getting a paint job that looked then, and still does, like cast glass. You were – and still are – just stunning!

I always wondered how good a Z could be. You are my answer.

I remember taking you to various car shows, where you either won or placed second in your class against some pretty good competition. But you were never only just a show car — you were always built to drive, first and foremost. You are still the best driving car I ever owned.

And what about that time driving down a street in Salem, when we came to a stop light and a car full of young men pulled up alongside, their windows went down and phones came out to take pictures. At the next light, they asked what you were. I told them a 1978 280Z. "Wow — I've never seen one before. That's older than I am!" Exactly.

In recent years, you've spent a lot of time under a cover in the shop, and I haven't done much with you. I haven't come up with anything I could do that would suit me more than what you are now. It's a rarity in the car hobby for a car to be done. You have been.

I had thought about getting to 40 years with you, but that's just an arbitrary number. No reason to hold out.

Painted, but not buffed

Because there came that day, late last year, when this happened:

(October 29, 2016) A lovely sunny and dry late fall day. I took you out for a longish drive prior to putting you away for the winter. Filled up with non-ethanol gasoline, put in Sta-Bil and a can of Seafoam, then drove around for maybe 40 miles.

You got a lot of looks, horn honks, thumbs-up and conversations waiting in line at stop lights. That happens a lot — even at car shows. But I have a sense that I was finding a way to part with you – that this might well have been my last real pleasure drive with you.

I considered that there is now nothing I would or could do to make you better than you have been for the last 2-3 years. I know full well that the experience will not get any better.

I have one more car to finish, and it will be every bit as good, but the experience will not last as long.

Trophies and awards

Someone else should have the chance to enjoy you. They will, I am sure. I will miss you. A gearhead friend says I will regret doing this. But I'm really OK with it. The sense is not regret. It's just a quiet internal sense that your story should continue with someone else. I'm pleased you won't be around here on local roads to remind me. You will be seen and talked about, probably show up in some shows I could never take you to, and be admired by a new group of interesting people.

It's time.

Thanks for 39 really great years.

21

VERA'S STORY

My mother wasn't at all happy about telephoning Rolls-Royce to apologise: "Hello? Yes, you have kindly written agreeing to bring a car to our home for my son to test with a view to buying it. Yes, that's correct, but I have to advise you that my son is only 11 years old!"

It was yet another example of how my naughty brother Dick's car-mad obsession got him into trouble. And Rolls-Royce did nothing to hold Dick's passion in check, since they incredibly kindly agreed to bring a car for him anyway, and to take him for the drive of his young life.

In fact it was ultimately a good move by Rolls-Royce since Dick went on to own many Rolls-Royces in his 97 years!

My father, on the other hand, never drove a car. But he must have been a mad-keen motorcycle enthusiast at one time, because before the First World War, he bought a Rex racing machine and he and his friend (on another fast bike) set out from Newport Pagnell to see the Isle of Man TT races.

This was at a time when roads were largely unmade and any journey longer than a few miles was rarely undertaken. Yet the two boys and their exotic machinery made it all the way to Liverpool, across on the ferry to Douglas, a distance of around 300 miles. And then all the way back to Newport Pagnell after the event. Incredible – a bit like driving from Paris to Peking today I should think.

Dick's 1933 Rolls-Royce 40/50hp Phantom II
Continental Sedanca Coupe at Turvey Garage

And the same car, sold by Bonhams for £234,700 in 2006

As soon as he was old enough, Dick bought his own motorcycle, and he and his friend Reg also acquired a BSA with a third wheel and a light van-type body with the front wheel sticking out the front, into which they loaded small rechargeable batteries.

Back then, many houses only had gas power, no electricity, and most of us were keen radio listeners. All the radios were powered by small rechargeable batteries which we called accumulators, and these needed recharging each week. So Dick and Reg started a little business collecting the exhausted batteries and replacing them with a fresh one, for a few pennies each week. That was to grow into a substantial garage business, eventually providing Dick and Reg with any car they fancied owning.

However, that was a long time in the future. For now, anything with two or four wheels and an engine was an object of desire. Remember that most people would cycle the six miles from

Turvey to Bedford, and lorries were so slow that cyclists would grab the tail of a passing lorry and hitch a tow. Sometimes you'd see half a dozen cyclists holding on to the back of a lorry for a bit of pedal-free assistance, and if one cyclist took a tumble he'd more than likely take the rest with him.

This was illegal of course, and relied on the lorry driver not spotting in his mirror what was going on behind his vehicle!

So when Reg bought himself a baby Austin 7 with a chrome radiator he was king of the hill in the village. This was a cheap and very small car, and Reg was a huge man, so it did look a bit comical. Reg didn't mind though, and he loved to show off his tricks with the car. One day he gave my mother a lift home, and decided it would impress her if he drove at speed along Bridge Street with his head sticking out of the sun roof, steering with his knees. Poor mum was so scared that as soon as she arrived home in one piece she burst into tears of relief.

We used to do amazing journeys in those old cars. Prescott hill climb in Gloucestershire was a very popular destination to see all the top racers and all the best cars such as Bugattis. It was a long way and took many hours, but four of us used to squeeze in to whichever car was available and we'd take off at top speed, determined to break the record for the trip.

Dick, Reg and their friend John with their rally Ford Anglia and trophies

After the races we'd return home, probably even faster. That's what you call a day's motoring!

One day, Dick took the Austin all the way to Pontypool in South Wales to see his girlfriend's family. That's maybe a 400 mile round trip. So the next day we decided we needed to show him that we could do marathon motoring just as well and four of us piled into our friend Jack's Austin and many hours at a steady 40-45 mph eventually got us there.

Then, after tea and cakes, we drove home!

Dick Geary with a new 1937 Ford 8

We moved into the big time when my fiancé was able to borrow his father's pre-War Packard. This was a big 8-cylinder American drop head that looked a million dollars. Stylish didn't come near to describing how this car looked, especially in the Britain of the late 1940s. However, it was pretty hopeless around town ... for a start there were no parking spaces big enough for the car!

When his mother needed to be driven around she always chose the Packard with her son as chauffer – despite having a good car of her own. She was very grand and demanded that he park right outside any shop she chose to visit. There used to be a high class fruit and veg shop near the railway bridge in Bedford, and parking the Packard there while she

was inside caused traffic mayhem. My fiancé was convinced he would be arrested and prosecuted but he was more scared of his mother than any policeman, so he did as he was told!

My fiancé and I much preferred travelling on his Sunbeam S8 motorcycle. He was working at Vincent's at the time with his friend John Surtees, who went on to be the only person ever to be world champion on two wheels and four. But of course no employee – other than John whose father was a Vincent dealer – could ever afford to buy this 'fastest motorcycle in the world'.

When we were married and our son came along, we simply bought a sidecar for the Sunbeam and the carry cot with baby travelled in that.

No wonder our baby grew up to love bikes and cars!

In many ways those were carefree times. Dick and Reg used to look after the MG PA belonging to Richard Shuttleworth's girlfriend.

Richard was a local hero; at the age of 23 he owned a fabulous stately home and a collection of sports and racing cars. When the authorities at Cambridge University told him that undergraduates were not allowed space to park a car, he simply bought an aeroplane!

Of course, the Shuttleworth Collection of cars and aeroplanes at Old Warden is now world famous and well worth a visit! Anyway, this young lady brought in her MG PA which was a very fast car by 1930's standards. One day the lads were testing the car after servicing it, when they picked up a police car tailing them. In those days I believe they needed to physically stop you to serve a summons, so the naughty boys contemplated powering away from the old police saloon.

Then – clearly no better behaved than back when Dick was 11 – he came up with a better plan. As a skilled mechanic he knew that the old rural police cars with white metal bearings couldn't cope with sustained high speed running. So instead of taking the MG up to 75 mph to prove his superiority and watch the police give up, he only increased his speed very gradually.

At 45 the police car was still there. Ditto 50. Then 60, which is where he held it, with bursts up to 70 and then falling back. "Yes", thought the policeman, "I can still just catch them!"

This went on for a few miles, exactly as Dick planned, before the police car suddenly emitted plumes of blue smoke and coasted to a standstill, its engine ruined! What a naughty brother!

My brother became an MG, Triumph and Jaguar dealer so we had lots of MG experiences, and I do remember one more crazy MG story involving my brother. In the early '70s he completed a full restoration of a customer's MG TC. It took a long time but it turned out like new and the car was duly

Top, Vera on the Sunbeam in the '50s, and below, on her very similar machine today!

parked at the side of the garage in Kempston on the Saturday that the car was being collected by its proud owner. That afternoon the owner arrived and was escorted to see his car. As they rounded the corner the sight that met their eyes left them speechless. The car was partly crushed; in far worse condition than when it was first brought in for its rebuild.

What had happened? Well, also at the end of the garage was a diesel pump and presumably a lorry had chosen to reverse in so as to turn around, and didn't see the diminutive MG in his mirror. Unsurprisingly, he chose not to advise anyone of what he must have known he'd done, and simply drove away.

The MG was once again rebuilt as new, but at a big financial loss to my brother's insurance company …

When Dick was 90, my son arrived at his house in a vintage Bentley. This was a racing car with a particularly difficult gearbox, even by the standards of 'crash' boxes. Something, I believe, called a constant-mesh or dog box requiring lots of practice and precision. My brother took the wheel and drove the Bentley just as well as he did at 25. His changes up and down the gears were perfect, just as if he'd known the car all his life.

We spend the first 20 years of our lives learning the basics, and after that it's all about gaining 'experience'.

That experience never leaves you, and increasing age just makes you get better.

22

COOPERS

My first experience of Cooper racing cars was at the wheel of a '50s F3 powered by a very highly tuned Norton Manx 'Double Knocker' motor much like the car that Stirling Moss raced in the early days of his career, towed to the tracks behind his father's Rolls-Royce.

The Norton Manx was the engine to have in 500 racing. Official output was about 50 bhp, 10% more than the rival JAP 500 but specialist tuners managed significantly greater figures. The downside was – and still is – the much higher cost.

The Manx was originally designed in 1927 and in 1938 the valve gear operation was modified to "double knocker" form. We had all the best developments in the Cooper I was fortunate to drive, including a combined, forged, main shaft and flywheel, additional piston rings, and an all-aluminium head and extra-short stroke for better revving.

Running on methanol, we were required to carry an orange sticker on the car because methanol burns with a clear flame so marshals needed to beware. This car was a lot of fun and very fast. Although at peak revs the vibration did tend to vibrate my eyeballs in their sockets, making my vision blurred until I snatched a higher gear!

It was a tricky car – starting needed several chaps to pull the car onto its compression stroke and then run, pushing like mad. When I popped the

clutch and (hopefully) it fired, the idea was to slow the car with the hand-brake so as not to collide with the inevitable half-asleep paddock spectator walking backwards into my path, while blipping the engine with the right foot to keep it running, left foot on the clutch and, when one came to a standstill, not forgetting that since the fuel pump was driven by a cam on the axle it only worked when moving, so I had to keep pumping the fuel lever else the motor would stall.

If any of these tasks was forgotten and the motor allowed to stop, the poor pit crew would have to go through the ritual again ... which didn't make the driver very popular!

One indication of the camaraderie of fellow competitors comes from the day when we failed noise test at one venue. The motor was LOUD – and without a more restrictive silencer I was banned.

Instead of welcoming my exclusion as an even better chance for others to win, fellow competitors enlisted the help of a friend with fireproof gloves

to quickly remove the silencer from one car when the driver returned to the paddock and rapidly mount it on my car to ensure that I got a run. Lovely people.

John Cooper himself was such a super gentleman, he took a great interest in the historics that bore his name and he used to ring me on Sunday evenings to check how we'd all got on that weekend – it was a real honour to 'Fly the Cooper flag' for him.

We had a lot of fun with the little F3, moving on to a 60s Junior, then a later F3 which we later brought up to F1 spec with a BRM engine, followed by a short time in a Cooper Bristol F2, and then memorable big races in genuine historic rear engine F1 Coopers which were fast and tricky but rewarding – until the day a very inexperienced driver came rocketing flat out right from the back, past everyone. He obviously didn't have a snowball in hell's chance of making the turn and took me out while I was battling for third. That was a nasty crash and damaged me as well as the car, and the repairs to my own chassis are still work in progress!

23

MASERATI 250F

"Stirling Moss has suggested that you drive the Maserati"

As wind-ups go, this appeared to be a particularly cruel one, involving both my friend and motor racing hero and my dream post-War front-engined Grand Prix car. So my response was rather less than effusive.

The caller clearly thought I needed persuading, so made it clear that I wouldn't be put to any trouble – I would be flown out to the South of

France, accommodated, then race in the Grand Prix retro, and finally flown home again in time for dinner on Sunday.

It was only now that the penny dropped and I considered that the offer could be genuine.

This was one of the short-chassis 'piccolo' cars, raced by Stirling who, it appeared, would be otherwise engaged at Laguna Seca and hence unable to drive the Maserati.

A mixture of disbelief, joy and terror followed. This must have been a multi-million pound car even back then, with a performance well out of my comfort zone.

"Ok," I muttered, "but I must have some time with the car in England for seat fitting and testing to get comfortable and familiarise myself with it before attempting to qualify at an historic continental Grand Prix."

I was assured that the car would be ready in good time, the Colotti transaxle was almost ready, and I would be called to be introduced to the car 'very soon'.

Well, the Colotti was delayed, various dates to try the car were postponed, and I when I boarded the aeroplane carrying my helmet and overalls I faced the prospect that my first opportunity to even sit in this legendary machine would be in the morning of qualifying. I remember being told that 'nausea' is simply another word for excitement'. I'm not sure I believed that now.

But Stirling once told me that the day I did not feel a touch of butterflies was the day something bad could happen since I would be too relaxed.

Coming from the Maestro himself I've never forgotten that sage advice. See a bit of 'stage fright' in a positive way as your mind 'concentrating' and preparing for what lies ahead.

In fact the butterflies were well-founded – there was a torrential downpour during qualifying and I spun this immensely powerful car, finally coming to rest on the infield grass to be joined seconds later by another 250F (driven by a famous racer, so that made me feel better about my own driving error!)

The car was brought back to the paddock, dripping wet and covered in mud, the owner looking mightily relieved that I'd not smashed up his beloved car. And as I hung up my soaking wet overalls to dry out a bit I was amazed to be told that I'd somehow managed to put in one lap that was fast enough to grab a reasonable spot on the grid.

That night was rather sleepless, but I need not have worried. As so often happens in the south of France after a downpour, the next day dawned warm and sunny, and track conditions were perfect. My overalls were almost dry – always a big bonus – and the car looked pristine, having been immaculately prepared by the top mechanics from Neil Davies Racing.

Finally getting to drive the Maserati in the dry was a revelation, a sheer joy. Since it was someone else's car I was not quite as brave as I wanted to be through the sharp turns, allowing one or two of the smaller cars to nip past, but as soon as I could see the exit I simply opened the taps and let the car take me past them again as if I was being fired from a cannon.

Just pure acceleration all the way to maybe 185mph. The brakes were very powerful; I remember them easily overwhelming the skinny cross ply tyres and locking up into corners the first few times. But I soon worked out that being able to see the tread pattern at 120mph on the approach was not a good thing, and I adjusted my pressure accordingly! Thanks to a well-prepared motor car and the fact that one or two better drivers went out with car failures, I ended the day on the podium and with an experience never to be forgotten.

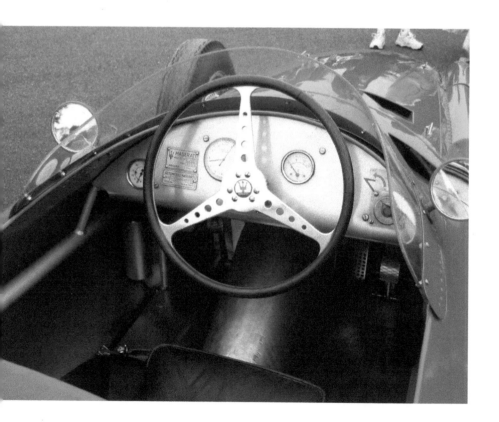

24

MORGAN'S 3 WHEELER

"Here's another story from Neil Furber, this time about Morgan's decision to launch a new version of their famous 1930s sports three-wheeler!"

If you're into bikes but not keen on using them on the public road, I might have found a solution. Morgan's 3 Wheeler!

I popped in to visit my friends at Allon White Sports Cars to buy a new pair of 'throttle-blippers' (some *Piloti Campione* driving boots). After a bit of trialling between a couple of sizes and confirming I wanted polished leather instead of suede I had made up my mind. But I needed to 'road-test' them. A couple of minutes later and I had the keys to their 3 Wheeler demon-

strator. I had been out in this car quite a bit during an event a few weeks previously but always in the wrong seat. This time I was in the right one! With the sun working its magic, luckily I had my *3-wheeler* cap with me.

The 3 Wheeler doesn't have adjustable seats. Instead, the pedal box can be unbolted and moved to suit the driver.

This all takes a little too much time for a short run out so I gratefully accepted the offer of their new packer cushion. Trimmed in beautiful black Napa leather by Allon White's in-house trim shop, it looked great. But it didn't match the brown interior! Ah, but there is a plan. The car is about to undergo a full interior re-trim in the black leather.

Climbing aboard, I draw on my old gymnastics skills to avoid kicking or scuffing the interior (or my new footwear!) and strapping-in I find the seatbelt over the *wrong* shoulder. With one click of the key and a sustained press on the starter button, the 2.0 litre S&S V-twin motorcycle engine grumbles into life.

A quick check on the floor-mounted pedals confirms the car has a race-car-style pedal-box and the new 'blippers' do exactly that with a nice heel & toe action. The very reclined driving position with this pedal-and-cushion setup means I have to sit bolt upright in my 'meerkat' pose for manoeuvring the car out of the car park. The pedals are all very direct and need smooth, delicate driver inputs for a nice clean pull away. I release the quirky fly-off handbrake and off we go!

With only two cylinders, the 3 Wheeler's engine isn't the smoothest at low speeds and needs to be driven differently to most cars. Through the villages, it's chomping at the bit when the engine is in the right speed range to be smooth. Shifting up to drop the revs makes the car want to bog down and shake the chassis so the lower gear seemed to work better. Another chance to test the new throttle-blippers! The engine makes a fabulous growl during the rhythmic pedal-dance of a double declutch downshift. Oh, back to chomping at the bit. Nearly reached the open road ...

The combination of driving position, wheel layout, body shape and teeny-tiny mirrors makes judging the distance to the kerb a little bit of an ongoing game during passing oncoming traffic and parked cars. Up to *meerkat* position, back to *reclined* position. Up to *meerkat*, back down again.

In the reclined position there is a sight line between the top of the steering wheel and the top of the bodywork. Conveniently fully behind the aeroscreen to keep the flies out of the teeth! In hindsight, moving the pedalbox would have been worthwhile but the spanners are back in the workshop. Plus I'm already having too much fun!

On first impression, the indicators seem to have a mind of their own but actually flicking them a second time in the same direction cancels the previous flashes. The lights and horn have nice weighty aluminium switches. The speedo is easy to see but would be completely hidden by a half-tonneau during rainy motoring. The tacho is half hidden behind the steering wheel rim but this engine needs to be driven on sound, not vision! The narrow chassis won't suit everyone but is great to brace during spirited driving. The left knee rests nicely against a padded leather gearbox tunnel.

Oh, here come the national speed limit signs. And ... off we go! The engine is torquey and wants to pull. From 3000rpm it becomes smoother and really starts to go. Blimey, 60 already! The first bend is coming up. On the brakes early, two throttle-blipping-double-declutching growls, in we go.

Hmm, the steering feels interesting. Not exactly vague but not really weighting up either. We'll come back to that. Up through the gears. Rolling on the throttle, up a gear. Rolling on again, up again. It drives just like my uncle's Harley felt from the back seat. But then the S&S engine is essentially a Harley-Davidson unit!

The steering is chattering away but not actually pulling side to side with appreciable bump-steer. Elbow in the chassis or outside? Yes, outside feels better. This must be how Fangio and the boys felt back in the day – simple chassis, exposed to the elements, no major crash protection. But brilliant fun!

Down to the T-junction, back on the brakes. A little later this time, let's see what they've got. Hmm, pretty good actually. There's more than I'd ever want to rely on for road driving. Yep, clear both ways let's go. A little chirp from the rear tyre as we pull out. I suppose it is very light with only one rear wheel and even that isn't very wide. Remember that! Rolling on the throttle and up a gear again. Does this little 3 Wheeler need more power? No. Should it have less power? Probably not – it's just too much fun! Oh, 60 again! This is the most engaging car I've driven in some time. Perhaps ever. It's keeping me on my toes and even when not actually going fast it feels a hell of a lot faster. Woooooah, big bump, the chassis didn't like that one, a shaky wobble, the big 3-spoke steering wheel gives a little jiggle but we're composed again. Fangio and the boys really did have a different era!

Okay, next turn on the left. Back on those confidence-inspiring brakes, new blippers back in action. (Pleased with those!) Pushing the chassis a little harder now, a hint of understeer and that funny front end feeling. Back on the power early sorts it out. The tail wakes up, that single rear tyre easily overpowered just enough to get the car turning-in but without becoming a real handful. Up a gear. This is a cracking little car – what a hoot! It feels like I've gone back in time and should be wearing a flying jacket and goggles. Come on Mr. Toad, poop poop!

Nearly back to the dealership. Oh just one more loop of the wiggly bit before we go back. Why not? A little quicker this time. Blimey, it really is quick actually. Properly quick in fact. It's meant to do 0-60 in about 6 seconds, but most of that seems to be the pull in 2nd gear. It certainly doesn't need any more power. Into the village, here come the speed bumps. And I'm not even annoyed – they're another blipping opportunity. Double-declutch-pedal-dance into 1st. Back up to 2nd. Brakes and pedal dancing again for the next one. My new friend is turning a few heads. I'm grinning like an idiot! In fact, I think I've looked like this since I pulled off. This car is infectious!

I thought the shoes were expensive, but they might be the cheapest purchase today!

LAGONDA MEMORIES

When I was a boy one of our top UK film stars was Kenneth More. He played everything from war heroes to inept comedy doctors, and he was one of the stars of my favourite film 'Geneviève' – which you've probably never heard of!

But it's worth watching – a quintessentially British tale of two Veteran cars racing from London to Brighton.

Kenneth is the fellow front left in the poster looking, it must be admitted, much as I did at the same age, complete with moleskin cap, tweed jacket and bow tie!

Anyhow, the British film industry wasn't like Hollywood, and if one had a vintage car as a prop then I have it on very good authority from Kenneth's friend that one stood more chance of landing a role over actors without such inducements!

Kenneth's daily car was a 1934 Lagonda Rapide sports in British

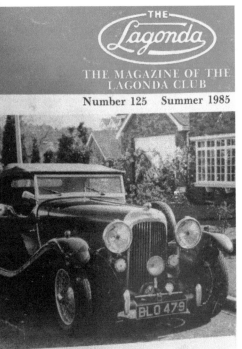

racing green with green leather. It was the Medical Officer's staff car at RAF White Waltham from '38-'45.

As a boy I remember thrilling to the sight of it in a film, loaded with maybe six medical students and a kidnapped stuffed gorilla stolen from a rival university, screeching around London in a car chase!

That car became mine when I was 27 (costing more than a new Ferrari so I must have been a very odd young man to choose such a car) and my children and I loved it, cared for it and enjoyed it for many happy years.

Sadly I stupidly agreed to sell it to a lawyer who then sued me some time later when it dropped a valve as he was driving out of Paris – yes, he had been touring Europe – claiming I had guaranteed that the car would *never* give him any reliability problems. And the judge believed him and made me pay the cost of an engine rebuild, which he had wrecked by both driving back to Birmingham UK and then removing the cylinder head himself ... ah well, all water under the bridge now.

26

THE DAY WAS
'LESS THAN SUCCESSFUL'

I've yet to find anyone who has been around cars for a few years who doesn't have a tale to tell. It might be of things your father told you (both wisdom and rubbish!) or your own skinned knuckles and dropped spanners trying to get the thing fixed so you could get yourself to work or college.

In common with most of us back then, much of my early car mainte-nance was done *al fresco*, often with a biting north wind as accompaniment. I may not have had a very good heater in my old Ford, but believe me, when I got that engine started and slipped behind the wheel it felt like a toasty reward!

A few years later I started motor racing, and I was at a race event many years ago, with a single seater car, when 'an old boy' shuffled up to me. "That's the wrong engine in that car y'know," he piped up.

"Hello", I said, already being used to this type of introduction from spectators.

"Yes, it would have originally been a small Ford engine from an Anglia like in the Harry Potter film, but it's been uprated." The lovely old chap chat-ted amiably for a few minutes and then moved on to share his knowledge with the next driver.

A month later, my 'phone rang. "Hello," came the broad Gloucestershire accent, "I've got that engine for you. Give me the money when you can, OK?"

"I'm sorry, who is this?"

"We met a while ago boy, and I told you that you had the wrong engine. Well I've sorted it for you. I met a bloke with the right engine so I bought it for you. No need to thank me, that's OK."

I came off the 'phone a bit shocked. What was that all about?

A few months went by and the 'phone rang again.

"You need to pick up that engine. The bloke wants it gone."

"Hello, who's this ...? Oh yes, I remember. Ummm, let me be honest, I don't really need an old engine, so can I just send you the money and whatever you want for yourself please, and we'll just forget about it?"

"It's not that simple," he said. "I have a bad back, and it HAS to be collected, so you'll have to get it yourself."

"OK," I sighed, "I'll come down in my Jaguar – I should be able to get the engine in the big boot. Where is it please?"

"It's not that simple," he said again. "The engine is still in the car."

"What???? You're kidding me. Where is it, by the way?"

"Abergavenny."

And so it was that I set out early the following day, having booked a day's precious holiday, in a 4X4 with a car trailer *en route* to Wales. When

I arrived, there was the rusty old Anglia, about 100 yards along a grassy, muddy track accessed through a field gate. It was on four flat tyres and looked as if it hadn't moved since the '70s.

How could this nightmare be happening? I winched the wreck on to the trailer and off I went again towards home. After an hour or so I stopped for fuel, and realised that this thing was never going to look good on my lawn. So I called my local garage. "Please help me," I begged. "I'll explain later but I need to drop off a Ford Anglia in your yard while we sort out getting it scrapped."

The kind garage man agreed to wait for me and at 7pm I rolled into the yard with the banger. "Why on earth have you bought this?" was the obvious question. "It's a long story," I started, "but essentially it's all about the original engine which is apparently fairly rare these days."

"Forget that," said the garage man, surveying the scene beneath the bonnet. "The original engine has gone, this is a bigger engine like the one you already have. Surely you checked when you picked it up?"

Well, of course, I hadn't had I? Ever had a bad day suddenly get worse?

ABOUT THE EDITOR

Richard McCann has spent a lifetime collecting, restoring and racing many exciting vintage and classic sports cars and racing cars.

In this book he brings together a collection of stories from the 1920s to the present day, involving the exploits of enthusiasts from all walks of life – but all 'car crazy' and each with a great tale to tell!

Lightning Source UK Ltd.
Milton Keynes UK
UKHW020206051221
394962UK00006B/140